Navajo

A small silver model of a U.S. army canteen of a type used during the Civil War. From the Gen. Charles McC. Reeve Collection, Southwest Museum. Two and a half inches in diameter.

A brief history

of Navajo silversmithing

by ARTHUR WOODWARD

Silver

NORTHLAND PRESS / FLAGSTAFF

This Book Originally Published
by
The Museum of Northern Arizona in August 1938
as Museum of Northern Arizona Bulletin No. 14

FIFTH PRINTING
January 1975

ISBN 0-87358-088-5
Library of Congress Catalog Card Number 74-174997

Contents

Illustrations

Foreword

IN 1938 THE MUSEUM OF NORTHERN ARIZONA published Bulletin Number 14, *A Brief History of Navajo Silversmithing,* by Arthur Woodward, curator of history at the Los Angeles Museum and a noted historian and archaeologist. Woodward's book summarized the history of silversmithing up to that date among the Navajo tribe, and for the first time, shed light upon the origins of some of their typical ornaments.

Few volumes on Navajo silversmithing were published prior to 1930, and since 1940 only about thirty articles and books on the subject have appeared. Among the latter, Woodward is frequently quoted and relied on for his part in uncovering the history of this Navajo craft. He was the first to present a comprehensive view of the *four* major influences on Navajo design, showing how the silversmiths adapted the art forms of European settlers and Indians in the eastern United States, as well as those of the Spanish and Mexican colonists of the Southwest.

In recent years, Navajo silver has become an important item of Indian art and craft work sold in shops from the East to the West Coast. It has become so popular that cheap imitations are manufactured in Japan in factories devoted to production of inexpensive curios. Authentic early examples of the craft have become treasured parts of both private and museum collections.

Navajo silversmithing has indeed come of age since Woodward's book was published.

This classic volume, one of the first and best reports on the craft, is among the most requested Museum publications. It has been out of print for more than five years. When the Northland Press proposed republishing *A Brief History of Navajo Silversmithing* in a more up-to-date format, we were pleased to offer our assistance.

This edition does not include new information, other than an updated addition to the bibliography, since for those who want to know more about the early history of this craft, it can be found here.

The jewelry, other than where noted, is in the Museum of Northern Arizona's collection and was especially photographed for this edition.

EDWARD B. DANSON
Director, Museum of Northern Arizona

Introduction

IN WRITING THIS BOOK no attempt has been made to enter into a technical discussion of the silversmith's craft among the Navajo. It is not intended to be a complete and final analysis of the art as practiced by those tribesmen. Such a book cannot be written until the last silversmith is dead and the production of silverware ceases.

My purpose is to summarize the history of the introduction of silversmithing among the Navajo and to attempt to cast some light upon the origins of certain of the ornaments made by native Navajo smiths.

Like all things it must have a beginning. Navajo silversmithing did not "just grow." We know it to be an alien art. We know that the earliest forms of Navajo jewelry were not indigenous. Hence at the outset we must cast about for logical prototypes of such forms. We must also follow the clues leading to the introduction of metal-working among these wandering desert dwellers.

In the past, a great deal of emphasis has been thrown upon Mexican silversmiths, who presumably taught the rudiments of the craft to the Navajo. However, aside from a few late statements, made by white traders in the 1880s, we have had no definite dates for the appearance of the first white silversmiths in the Navajo country. Similarly the ornaments themselves have been looked upon as having Mexican origins. In this book I propose to show the part played by the Mexican influences and also to bring into proper focus the other stimuli of entirely different character. To do this it will be necessary to leave the Southwest and travel into the Eastern woodland areas, where European silver ornaments were first introduced by fur traders during the middle of the eighteenth century, in order to show how that trade later influenced the Navajo craft in the middle of the nineteenth century.

Hence, before undertaking the final analysis of the ornament forms as ultimately accepted and developed by Navajo smiths it will be necessary to paint in the general background of both the Eastern and Southwestern influences. Since the art and some of the forms under discussion first originated among the Indians of the eastern part of the United States, I propose to review somewhat briefly the introduction, spread, and subsequent native manufacture of silver jewelry in that area, prior to discussing the Spanish-Mexican contributions.

1: Eastern Phases of the Craft

THE USE OF SILVER OBJECTS among the following tribes[1] began about 1740: Iroquois, Delaware, Micmac, Cherokee, Alibamu, Shawnee, Choctaw, Creek, Yuchi, Penobscot, Kickapoo, Koasati, Miami, Ottawa, Huron, Wea, Pottawatomi, Illinois, Ojibwa, Sauk, Fox, Iowa, and Seminole. Of this group the Iroquois, Delaware, Shawnee, Illinois, Cherokee, Kickapoo, Miami, Ottawa, Huron, Wea, Pottawatomi, and Ojibwa probably received the ornaments earlier than some of the others; that is, 1740 marks the approximate date of introduction among any of the tribesmen. In turn the various groups obtained the silver "toys," as the ornaments were noted on English trade lists, as the fur traders penetrated their respective tribal areas. Thus the Iroquois, Delaware, Ottawa, Shawnee and others with whom the longest trade contacts had been established received silver trade objects at the outset of their innovation and the others accepted the same type ornaments as the trading frontiers advanced.

Between 1740 and 1750 ornaments of good coin silver were

part of the stock of every successful fur trader. The silver flood that had swept over the Atlantic seaboard tribes had by this time begun to inundate the Ohio and Mississippi valleys and was flowing through the forest lands around the Great Lakes.

Prior to 1740 there were a few sporadic introductions of silver medals which were issued to particularly influential chiefs, but even those were not specially cast for the Indians, having been commemorative medals struck to celebrate British or French victories on the Continent.[2] Apparently the soft sheen of silver appealed to the Indians and it was not long before ornaments of the same metal made their appearance in fur traders' lists and upon the requisitions for governmental presents to be distributed to those tribes who "held fast to the silver chain of friendship," as ceremonial parlance of the day described such alliances.

Perhaps the absence of silver gewgaws for the Indians in the seventeenth and early part of the eighteenth centuries can be explained by the relative scarcity of the precious metal among the colonists in North America. Brass ornaments had been a stock in trade from the beginning, but ere long silver superseded the brass and the latter fell into the discard until a later date.

Competition between the British and French interests in their race for the domination of the fur trade called into play every possible means of winning over the Indians who owned the rich hunting grounds. During the French and Indian War, 1755–1763, the distribution of silver ornaments by traders and officials alike rose in an ever ascending scale.

The array grew from a few commemorative medals to a specialized assortment of brooches of many sizes, ranging from those the size of a dime to those as large as a small soup plate. Arm bands were graded according to width and decoration. Then there were gorgets, semilunar in shape, official and non-official; round gorgets of varying sizes and designs. There were highly ornamented crucifixes, some worn in clusters in the ears; others a foot long hung upon the breasts of Indians who had never seen the inside of a church. These were fashioned in a variety of forms ranging from the simple Latin cross through the more decorative patterns of the Patriarchal, Botonée, and Fleury, and the designs engraved thereon were sometimes far from being of a religious nature; hence, the implication that Indian burials found with silver crosses in them are those of Christian converts is likely to be erroneous. As far as I am aware, the early Jesuit missionaries of the seventeenth century did not distribute silver crucifixes to their charges. Small brass, iron, bronze or copper ones were all they could afford, and these are readily recognized when found. In addition to the ornaments mentioned were earrings, ear-bobs, ear-wheels, nose-rings, nose-bobs, hair-pipes, head-bands, hair-plates, and finger-rings, the latter being plain, engraved, or set with glass. The earrings were long pendants, short pendants, semilunar flat dangles with separate hinged centers, simple rings of silver wire, or thin loops of silver wire, bearing tear drop clusters of five to twenty tinkling silver cones, worn in each ear.

The Indians were not long in discriminating between thin, alloyed ornaments and those of coil silver.[3] (The latter were readily accepted as pawn by fur traders and government officials when the Indian owners were in need of credit for the purchase of needed goods.)

The traders obtained their stocks of silverware from both European and Colonial silversmiths. In Appendix No. 1 will be found a list of some of the men who are known to have turned their hand to this little-known phase of American silversmithing.

At the outset the bulk of these trinkets were of good coin silver, as I have already mentioned, and when one considers the itemized statements of fur traders and government officials concerning the number of silver ornaments that went into certain portions of the country in one year, the results are somewhat surprising, and give rise to speculations as to the ultimate fate of this glittering array of trinkets that showered down upon the woodland people during those eventful years.

For example, in 1767 in one British order of silver "toys" for the tribesmen in the neighborhood of Fort Pitt (now Pittsburgh, Pennsylvania), a total of 8,976 individual items were included in the list of presents destined to be distributed that year. There were arm bands by the twenty dozen; brooches, 300 dozen; ear-bobs, 50 dozen; crosses 20 dozen, etc.[4] Again in 1782, in the estimate of merchandise needed for Indian presents at Detroit for that year alone, the silver truck amounted to 18,600 specimens, while the ornaments destined for the post of Michillimackinac in the same year totaled 1,550, making a grand total of 19,150 pieces.[5] When one realizes that is only *one year's* distribution from two frontier posts, and when one further considers the fact that this same silver flood had inundated the country in varying degrees for some forty to fifty years previous to this time, the amount of money expended upon silver ornaments and the number of such ornaments distributed, is a bit staggering.

During the period of the American Revolution the fur trade languished somewhat, but at the same time a certain amount of "salve" was needed to anoint the feet of distant tribesmen to enable them to travel swiftly to the aid of the Great White Father who lived across the Big Water. Having the resources, the British were able to hold their Indian allies well in line by means of lavish gifts. The Americans had no gifts to send.

After the Revolution, the boundary disputes were prolonged chiefly to enable the British traders on the frontier, particularly in the Northwest, to drain the area of furs and get a firmer grip upon their Indian allies in that region.

It was at this point that the American traders entered the race and began competing with their British adversaries for domination in the newly acquired territories. In order to make this competition effective, the Americans were forced to adopt the same tactics employed by their rivals. Hence, the same quality of trade goods had to be purchased, the same system of medal and gorget giving practiced, and annuity payments of silver and goods made to those tribes with whom the young nation was forced to make treaties. Ironically enough, because of the lack of native American industries, the bulk of the trade goods used by private traders and those sold over the counters of United States factories, as trading posts were called, during the late 1790s and early 1800s were purchased abroad, chiefly in England, from wholesale concerns in Birmingham and Sheffield.

The opening of the West through the Lewis and Clark explorations, 1804–1806, and the rapid settlement of the trans-Allegheny region and what was then termed the Northwest Territory, forced the American trappers and traders to seek new fields. They left the old hunting grounds, now depleted, and entered upon a new era of trading among tribes that hitherto had been almost legendary.

The eastern Indians who had survived the ever encroaching white settlements, abandoned by the traders, yet having become accustomed to the white man's mode of living and dependent upon him for clothing, tools, weapons, ornaments, etc., were forced to follow the white man's road or die. One of the trades they learned was that of silversmithing and iron working. One cannot say definitely when active work in these metals began by those tribes. However, judging by all documentary and material evidences, it must have been in the late 1790s or soon after 1800. The people most efficient in silversmithing were the Iroquois, Delaware, Cherokee, Alibamu, and possibly the Shawnee. In 1809 there were 49 native Cherokee silversmiths turning out ornaments for their tribesmen and neighbors.[6] The most famous of these was Sequoyah, who turned from blacksmithing to silverworking, and is said to have stamped his wares, George Guess, Gist or Guest, the only native smith of his day, of whom I have any record, who marked his product in imitation of the white smiths.[7]

As early as 1789, some of the Delaware, by permisson of the Spanish government, moved into what is now Missouri and afterward to Kansas. With them went some Shawnee. By 1820 two bands of Delaware had found their way to Texas. There were 700 in that group. By 1835, most of the tribe was gathered in Kansas and in 1867 they moved to the Cherokee Nation in Oklahoma.[8] I doubt very much whether any other tribe ever traveled so extensively in such a short period as did those former tidewater Delaware from the Atlantic coast.

Nor did they abandon their material culture when they moved. Hence, it is not surprising that silversmithing, as practiced by the Delaware, should be taught by them to the Kiowa-Comanche men with whom they came in contact in Texas.

At the same time, the white traders who had crossed the Mississippi and worked gradually westward, out onto the Plains and into the Rocky Mountains, carried with them the same traditions of the trade that had been in vogue for more than two hundred years.

Certain of the more utilitarian objects such as cloth, blankets, guns, powder, lead, shot, kettles, axes, knives, sugar, coffee, liquor, etc., were readily acceptable to the western tribesmen. Glass beads were more in demand for the ornamentation of costumes than in the East, but wampum, that indispensable commodity of the trade in the seventeenth and eighteenth centuries, failed to gain a foothold although it was tentatively accepted by some of the Missouri tribes early in the nineteenth century but died a lingering death. On the other hand long shell beads, known to the trade as hair pipes, and manufactured in the Campbell Brothers wampum factory at Pascack, Bergen County, New Jersey, and another variety of Bahama conch shell "gorgets," made in the same factory, sold readily among the Dakota.[9] Silver ornaments too found favor, but not in the variety seen earlier in the trade. Bracelets, finger-rings, hat-bands, ear-bobs, solid brooches, and the circular gorgets were acceptable among the Sioux, but not among the tribes living further to the north and west. Those people preferred shell ornaments. Brass bracelets and finger-rings, plain and set with glass, were also restored to favor in this area.[10]

Good silver ornaments did not survive long in the Plains trade. The reason for this seems to be a combination of circumstances brought about by several different factors. In the first place the traders, in common with all of their ilk, sought to make as much profit out of the fur trade as they possibly could. However, conditions were different in the West than in the East. The Indians of the latter area had been the actual purveyors of valuable furs and, until the beaver, otter, marten, mink, muskrat, etc., had become scarce, had done most of the hunting and trapping. The white men had played but a relatively small part as the actual trappers of the game. Hence, aside from the Hudson's Bay Company in the Far North, the average Colonial trader dealt directly with the Indian in the field and did not maintain any large crew of white hunters.

West of the Mississippi the reverse was true. The Indians were not trappers. They hunted buffalo, deer, and antelope for hides and robes, and such skins were definitely less valuable than those of the almighty beaver. The latter animal was taken in steel traps by well organized companies of employees of large fur corporations, and a host of independent trappers, all of whom became famous as the Mountain Men.

Hence, one need not wonder at the drop in the quality of trade goods from about 1830 to the end of the fur trade, which in reality was already in the last stages of decline, and by 1850 was virtually a thing of the past in the Plains and Rocky Mountain region. For these reasons, the substitutions of various cheap metals, such as German silver, brass, and copper and later nickled brass, for the higher grade silver, is not surprising.

Thus we find German silver coming into its own during the 1830s among the northern and southern Plains people, and also accepted by the tribes living on the eastern edge of the plains and in the Rocky Mountains.[11]

Of the various ornaments adopted by the Plains tribes the bracelets, finger-rings, earrings, and large, round, solid or simply pierced brooches and hair ornaments were the only ones that persisted. The bracelets and finger-rings were retained and used in their original forms, but the hair plates, large, circular, slightly concave discs, and the huge brooches were adapted for other purposes.

Originally the hair plates were attached in a graduating string to the long false queue of hair affected by so many of the Plains tribes. Thus had these hair ornaments been worn in the East by some of the Cherokee, Delaware, and Shawnee. However, the Dakota, Crow, Cheyenne, Kiowa, Comanche, Ute, and possibly the Oto, Osage, and Omaha, wore these round discs and oval ornaments as hair decorations and also fastened to leather belts.[12] The women of the Plains favored such belts and at first glance one might easily mistake one of the early belts of this type for an early Navajo belt of similar pattern.

This in brief is a hasty glimpse at the origin and spread of silver ornaments and silver working from the eastern woodland to the Plains and Rocky Mountains. Because of the nature of this book, in that the art of Navajo silversmithing is the primary subject under discussion, further details of the various phases of eastern silverworking have no place herein. On the other hand, since certain of the ornament types as well as modes of decoration, as adopted and later manufactured by the Navajo, were direct copies of these eastern specimens, I deemed it necessary to introduce those ancestral prototypes prior to the discussion of the Navajo offspring.

2: Hispano-Mexican Influences

HAVING DELVED SOMEWHAT into one branch of the family of Navajo smithing, which has entailed a study of basic ornament forms rather than the actual mechanical processes involved in the production of Navajo wares, we now turn to the second main branch of the art.

To undertake a review of the elements contributed by the Spanish-Mexican culture one must seemingly digress more than in the exposition of the fur trade. The sources of the origins of certain of the Navajo ornaments, not covered in the preceding section, are more varied and hence the task of presenting a clear picture of the situation is not so easy. Perhaps the easiest approach to the problem is to indicate in a few preliminary paragraphs the basic factors, and depict these in detail in their proper place in the main body of the text devoted to these subjects.

Thus the discussion of the forms and usages of the numerous silver buttons in Navajo material culture will of a necessity include a review of Spanish-Mexican costumes. The same will hold true of the necklace beads, but on the other hand, the analysis of the *naja* or crescent shaped ornament worn as a complement to the necklace will be in an entirely different field.

We know that the Spaniard delighted in an ostentatious display of wealth, which often manifested itself in the personal adornment of his clothing, weapons, and horse trappings. This love of finery was not confined to any one class alone. It has been remarked that the Mexican dandy of the eighteenth and nineteenth centuries might not have a peso in his pocket, but his hat and clothes were profusely decorated with silver and gold, thus creating the impression that the wearer was a man of wealth and influence.[13]

Following the more elaborate gold and silver laced hats and coats of the eighteenth century came a period when the styles changed. The wide gold and silver galoon (a tape-like binding or trimming), although still in evidence, began to give way to narrower strips and a profusion of silver buttons.

The characteristic small clothes, i.e., short knee trousers and cutaway coats, began to be replaced by an ever lengthening pair of trousers, while frock coats and shell jackets (a semi-formal tight fitting jacket, short in the back), profusely ornamented with silver and gold thread embroidery, replaced the more pronounced Colonial type coats. By the opening of the third decade of the nineteenth century, long slashed trousers, open from ankle to hip, were in vogue in Mexico and had begun to find their way into the outlying provinces of New Mexico and California. The short trousers, while still somewhat in use among the old die-hards of fashion, soon disappeared from the general run of Mexican costumes and were seen only among the Indian tribes of New Mexico and Arizona, the Puebloan groups, and the Navajo.

The Navajo men adopted the short knee breeches; the *botas,* or knee length wrap-around leather leggings; the shoes with hard soles and soft tanned uppers, with the tips of the soles slightly upturned to guard the toes in the stirrups; the short cloth or leather jackets; and even the low-crowned broad-brimmed black felt hats; and some there were, who even imitated the club-like queue of hair wrapped with cloth or cord,[14] the typical hair dress of the Mexican man about 1750 onward until the opening decades of the nineteenth century. One might be tempted to go a bit further and wonder whether the so typical hair dress of the modern Navajo and Pueblo men is a modified form of this eighteenth century Spanish style.

At any rate we are certain of the costume adaptation. The soft buckskin leggings, shoes, and trousers were stained brick red or black, the two colors affected by the Spanish and which are still popular with the Southwest Indians today.

It has always seemed to me that the Navajo man is a living exponent of acculturation. He wears on his person in his various garments visible evidence of the accumulation of material culture from alien sources. First of all, a Navajo wears underneath his outer garments his native breech clout. This he does not remove, unless he takes a bath, and even then some of the men do not take it off. Over the breech clout is a pair of calico drawers fashioned rather fully and being slightly more than knee length. These are slit up the outer seam from the bottom for about six or seven inches. These were his pantaloons in the days when Mexican costume was in vogue. The Zuñi men still wear these eighteenth century cotton trousers which were affected by the lower classes in Mexico until well after 1850. The long trousers of similar cut are worn in Mexico today by the less well-to-do laborers.

Over the aboriginal and Spanish-Mexican garb the Navajo has placed his latest acquisitions, the American jeans, shirt, shoes, and hat. Thus we have in him a living exponent of three layers of culture; he has absorbed them all and discarded none.

So it was with him in the use of the silver ornaments on the Spanish-Mexican costume of the late eighteenth and early nineteenth centuries. He clung to the buckskin short clothes festooned with silver buttons along the outer seams of the trousers, on the jacket sleeves and front, and on the *botas*. Even after he abandoned the outer garments of the Spaniard for those of the new interloper, the American, the Navajo continued to use the buttons as ornaments.

The Navajo woman, prior to 1864–65, wore the old simple two-piece *poncho*-like homespun garment with the square shoulder *manta,* and the wrapped buckskin leggings and moccasins. The dress and shawl seem to be aboriginal, and as such they were not buttoned or decorated with ornaments. However, the bodice and skirt made of cloth, given the refugees at Bosque Redondo, patterned upon the full flowing skirts and bodices of the white woman of that day, afforded more excuse for the use of silver buttons, and so the women came into their own. It was not until after the American conquest that the spread of silver coins became prevalent in New Mexico. The few aristocrats of New Mexico had silver in a limited quantity when that country was opened up by the Santa Fe trade after 1812. However, the majority of the residents did not use silver as a medium of exchange,[15] hence the idea that Mexican silver was easily obtained by the Navajo for their jewelry is a bit erroneous. In later years, Mexican silver dollars did come into the country, at a lower rate of exchange, but even as the eastern tribesmen, who manufactured their own ornaments, used English and American small silver currency and demanded it in annuity payments, so did the Navajo fall back upon American coins for their supply.

These Spanish-Mexican costumes were profusely ornamented with buttons and other trinkets. The slash in the trouser legs increased as those garments lengthened. The knee length trousers were open along the outer seam of each leg for a distance of some six inches above the knee. These slits were fastened by four to six buttons which varied in shape and size. Some were flat and plain. Others were half round, while others, the most common variety, were ball buttons, attached to a short length of silver chain. Frequently additional ornaments fashioned to represent pomegranates dangled at the ends of silver chains near each hip. The shell jackets were trimmed with the usual complement of six buttons down the front and two upon each sleeve. These matched the trouser ornaments.

As previously noted, when the trousers increased in length there were from 19 to 24 buttons on each leg, in addition to which there were from two to four of the pomegranate ornaments on each hip. Likewise, the wide flap in the front of garments, somewhat resembling the cut of the U.S. sailor's uniform of today, was ornamented with four to six large, flat, circular buttons.

One of the first American accounts of the Navajos, published in 1824 (see Note 16, p. 66) describes the garb of a Navajo slain in battle. He was dressed in a Mexican outfit lavishly trimmed with silver buttons. Some of the earliest pictorial records of the Navajo and Pueblo Indians, drawn from Government reports in the 1840s and 1850s, show the leading Navajo men clad in the Indian adaptation of the Mexican short clothes of the late eighteenth and early nineteenth centuries. Photographs made during the 1860s and 1880s likewise indicate that the old style garments, replete from shoes and *botas* to shirts, all elaborately decorated with silver buttons, were still in vogue.

Moreover, the mode of wearing silver upon the garments was not the only extravagance practiced by some of the Spanish men. They trimmed their saddles and bridles with silver, which varied in style and pattern according to the period. To wit, in the 1820s, in Mexico, there came into vogue the practice of ornamenting saddle trees with the huge silver curtain tie-backs which were manufactured in Birmingham, England and exported to Mexico after 1824.[17] The head stalls, cheek straps and side plates of the bit were silver trimmed, *conchas* were favorite ornaments near the ears, while crescent shaped ornaments lay against the animal's forehead (see the discussion of this ornament under *naja*). All of these items contributed in one way or another to the later Navajo silversmithing.

Another source of design elements found on Navajo silver of today may be found in the elaborately stamped saddle leathers, the cantles, saddle skirts, *mochilas,* and *tapaderos.* These patterns were achieved by the use of small steel dies. The repeated elements found on the Mexican saddle leather of the early nineteenth century are identical with those encountered upon the general run of Navajo silver jewelry. Hence it seems fairly safe to assume that the first dies used by the Navajos were in reality Mexican leather punches.

3: History of the Craft

WHEN ONE CONSIDERS the section of the Navajo country in which silversmithing and iron working first obtained a definite foothold, one perceives that it is in the heart of the Navajo country, far removed from the immediate proximity of the Mexican-Spanish settlements.

If, as it has been assumed, wandering Mexican-Spanish *plateros* or silversmiths were responsible for the introduction of the craft among the Navajos, why did the Indians not learn the art of metal working in the previous centuries of contact with the Spanish? Is it not logical to suppose that if these wandering smiths had penetrated the interior of the Navajo country, and we know Spanish expeditions were among the Navajo and reported on them as early as 1742,[18] the Navajos would have been making and wearing a profusion of silver ornaments long before the American period? Moreover, does it not seem logical to suppose that such an art, if it had been introduced by the Spanish, would have flourished along the extreme eastern margin of the

Navajo country, at the contact points rather than far inland?

Any metal working craft cannot be learned by mere contact. It requires tools, material, and sufficient time for a novice to learn the trade, hence occasional contacts between sworn enemies, even during the peaceful lulls, would not suffice. A captive who knew how to work metals might teach others the trade, provided he had the tools and metal, and both of the latter were extremely scarce in the frontier settlements of New Spain.

The answers to these questions, I believe, are relatively simple. After the conquest of New Mexico by General Stephen Watts Kearny in 1846, and the subsequent continual warfare and active penetration of the Navajo hinterland by American troops, which ended with the final campaign of 1863–1864, the Navajo were gradually made to understand that the aggressiveness of the Americans was decidedly different than the almost passive acquiescence of the Mexicans.

During the first few years of the American occupation, the Navajo played a cat-and-mouse game with the newcomers. The Americans, on the other hand, not understanding the tribal organization of the Navajo, staged a comedy of errors. The military campaigns of 1846–1858 consisted of a series of punitive expeditions and treaties which made the American authorities the laughing stock of the Southwest. It was not until the Bosque Redondo episode that the Navajo really felt the weight of Uncle Sam's hand, and the blow dealt the tribesmen at that time was one they never forgot.

As a means of gaining a foothold in the heart of the Navajo country Fort Defiance was established at the conclusion of the 1851–1852 campaign. Thither, in the fall of 1853, repaired Captain Henry L. Dodge, newly-appointed Agent of the Navajo. He seems to have been a fair-minded man, and one who might have wielded some influence among the proud warriors of that tribe had he lived. His letters written to the editor of the *Santa Fe Weekly Gazette* concerning affairs in the Navajo country are particularly interesting, in that they are among our first descriptions of that region by one other than a commander of military troops.

In one letter written by Dodge to the *Gazette*, published in the issue of January 7, 1854, I believe we have the first definite *dated* reference to the establishment of a blacksmith and a silversmith in the very heart of the Navajo country. All other references to the appearance of Mexican smiths, or in fact any kind of a smith among the Navajo are made by men who appeared in that country as traders thirty years later. Shrewd surmises, based upon the statements of the latter men, have placed the introduction of the craft among the Navajo not earlier than 1850.

Dodge's letter is as follows:

Navajo Agency
Pass Washington
November 16, 1853

Mr. Editor:

I have established the Agency for the Navajos at this point, until the spring, or at least until Congress makes an appropriation for the building and permanent location of the Agency. The Governor, ex officio, Superintendent of Indian Affairs of this Territory, has recommended that an appropriation be made by this Congress, of five thousand dollars to be expended in making permanent residence for the Agents of the different tribes. I believe that you and I know enough of Indian character to say emphatically that an Agent can have but little influence unless he lives in the Indian country and has daily intercourse with the leading men of the nation.

I have with me George Carter who is their blacksmith, a man of sterling worth and every inch a soldier — a Mexican silversmith, an assistant, Juan Anea, my interpreter, and two Mexican servants.

Upon my arrival here the Indians expressed much surprise that I should come so far into their country to live, with so small a force. I answered them by exhibiting my Commission from the President with the great seal of the United States affixed, appointing me their agent, and had the Interpreter to tell them, that I was commanded by the Governor of the Territory and the President of the United States, to have the same care of them as if they were my relatives and friends, and that I had not the least fear of them whatever as my intentions were good in every way possible, and to keep them at peace with all nations; that they might kill me whenever they found I gave them bad advice or that I was an injury to them or their country. I would live in the settlements as their agent, I would tear up my commission or send it back to the great man of the United States that he might send them a man that would live among them and control their actions by good advice and watching over their interests.

They immediately replied, they were glad to see me particularly as I came without soldiers and that all of the good men of the nation, would protect me and my property, and would be governed by my advice in all things, but that they had bad men amongst them that were very hard to control, but hoped that my living with them might have a good effect upon the bad, for that I would become acquainted with them individually and could point them out, and if necessary have them punished.

HENRY L. DODGE
Indian Agent, For Navajos

Unfortunately Dodge did not live long enough to carry out his intentions of being godfather to the Navajo. He was killed by a band of Apache while on a hunting trip, thirty miles south of Zuñi, November 29, 1856. (See additional notes on this occurrence in the statement of Chee Dodge in the Appendix, supplied by Mr. Richard Van Valkenburgh.) A portion of his remains was found by a cavalry patrol under Lieutenants Carlise and Alley about 11 a.m., February 12, 1857 and carried back to Fort Defiance where it was interred in the post cemetery.[19]

However, by this time the seed of silver and iron working had been planted in the heart of the Navajo country.

In the following paragraphs, substantiated by dated documentary evidence and personal statements obtained in the field from Navajo informants by Mr. Van Valkenburgh in 1936–1937, I believe we can state with a fair degree of certainty that the Navajo learned silver, and possibly iron working, after 1853. In fact, the man who is indicated as being the first silversmith, known to the Navajo as Atsidi Sani (the Old Smith), to the Spanish as Herrero Delgadito (Little Lean Iron Worker), acquired his knowledge of silversmithing between 1853 and 1858, and may have had some rudimentary ideas of iron working, which Navajo history states he learned from a Mexican captive taken prisoner near Socorro probably a year or so prior to 1853.

Since all indications seems to point to Herrero as being the first Navajo to undertake the manufacture of silver ornaments it might be well to inquire into the meager accounts concerning his early history.

Shortly after the 21st of November, 1858, a man by the name of Herrero was elected "Head Chief" of the Navajo around Fort Defiance.[20] His selection came about as a result of a demand made upon the Navajo of that section by the United States military authorities, at the conclusion of a campaign waged against them by the Federal troops in the fall of that year. He was noted then as being "a young man of intelligence and wealth." Armijo, another Navajo, was also elected as a leader at the same time.

As far as I am aware at the present time, this is the first appearance of Herrero in the public eye. No mention of his prowess as a silversmith was mentioned at that time, but his Spanish name, Herrero, by which he was known to the Americans and the Spanish, seems to indicate that he might have already begun to work in iron. Although Navajo tradition ascribes this knowledge of working *bes* or iron to the Mexican captive, it must be remembered that George Carter, the American blacksmith, seemingly forgotten by the Navajo at this late date, had established his forge in "Pass Washington," five years before Herrero was created a headman. Moreover since a Mexican silversmith was working alongside Carter, it does not seem illogical to suppose that this unnamed smith (could he have been the Cassilio mentioned in later years?) was the one who taught Herrero Delgadito how to work *bes lahk ai* (white iron or silver). Chee Dodge, with whom Herrero lived for a long time, mentions in his statement that Herrero did go to the forges established by Captain Dodge and, according to Chee, he "looked on and learned some things."

At any rate both traditional and documentary evidence point to the "Old Smith" as being the "daddy of silversmiths" and in the light of subsequent testimony delivered by Herrero himself, there seems to be little doubt as to the accuracy of this statement.

It has been repeatedly stated that although the Navajo were wearing silver ornaments prior to the 1860s, there is no reference to the actual manufacture of such objects by the Indians themselves.

In 1855 Dr. Jonathan Letterman wrote a "Sketch of the Navajo Tribe of Indians, Territory of New Mexico,"[21] in which he described the arts, crafts, and costume of the Navajo. Speaking of the man's garb, he said:

"Over all is thrown a blanket, under and sometimes over

which is worn a belt to which are attached oval pieces of silver, plain or variously wrought."

He continued further and mentioned the style of the bridles. "The side and front parts generally consist of strings; sometimes made of pure silver, of the purity of which, by the way, these people are excellent judges."

In the latter part of September, 1858, a Zuñi scout attached to the United States troops killed a Navajo woman in the skirmish of Laguna Negra, headquarters of Zarcillos Largos (Long Earrings), a prominent leader of the recalcitrant tribesmen. From this woman the Zuñi "captured a silver belt worth $50 or $75 – also $100 or $200 worth of coral necklace, precious stones, and other articles greatly prized by the Indians and only possessed by the rich."[22]

The first representation of a Navajo wearing a belt I have been able to find is an illustration published by Lieutenant Ives in his report on the exploration of the Colorado River. This appears to be a narrow leather belt studded with oval silver *conchas*.[23] The date of the expedition was 1858.

It will be noted however, that although these early accounts mention the use of silver they do not refer to the manufacture of the ornaments by native smiths.

Therefore one may conclude that either the Navajo were not manufacturing their own trinkets at this early period of smithing, or else there was but a limited amount being made and the smiths so few that their workmanship had not yet fallen under the observation of the white recorders. I am inclined to accept the latter theory.

The year 1853 marks the first well-defined introduction of a silversmith into the region where the craft later became quite active. Herrero, the man accredited with being the first Navajo smith, is in the limelight in 1858, five years after the coming of the Mexican smith; and Herrero, in 1863, is accepted by white men and Indians alike as a full-fledged leader of his people and a recognized artisan in metals.

The tribesmen who surrendered in 1863 were first taken to Fort Canby, an outpost established beyond Fort Defiance, and to a sub-camp of Canby, known as Callitas, prior to being transported to Fort Sumner and the Bosque Redondo reservation. A correspondent stationed at Fort Canby during the campaign wrote to the *Rio Abajo Weekly Press,* at Albuquerque, February 23, 1864, mentioning the ability of the Navajo to rehabilitate themselves, and in the following words presents the first definite information I have been able to uncover concerning the actual manufacture of silver ornaments by the Navajo at that period. . . . "the warriors themselves fabricate saddles, and bridles, and buckles, buttons and clasps of silver which are tasteful ornaments to their finely fitting cloth and buckskin dresses."

His statements were corroborated later in the same year by another unnamed correspondent, presumably an army officer, who wrote to the editor of the *Army and Navy Journal,* November 5, 1864, concerning the Navajo then at Bosque Redondo:

"They also manufacture silver ornaments of a very creditable style of workmanship."

However, it would not seem that the output was very great, nor, in the light of subsequent studies of actual specimens and the examination of photographs made of Navajo prisoners at that time, very extensive insofar as variety was concerned.

The testimony of Herrero himself, as delivered through the interpreter, Epifano Vigil, at Bosque Redondo, June 27, 1865,[24] concerning the mechanical abilities of himself and his people is more than interesting. The statement is as follows:

"Herrero and Armijo are the two principal chiefs of the Navajo Nation. Herrero has been a chief for a good many years.

. . . Herrero has not numbered his people; does not know how many are present on the reservation; does not know how many are in their old country, but there are three bands, under chiefs Manuelito, Herrero, and Yutachiquito – Herrero is a cousin of the head chief present."

Continuing his questioning Vigil elicited the following information from Herrero:

"Don't know whether the young men could repair the ploughs or not; is a blacksmith, and from him some of the young men have learned. Herrero Delgadito works in iron – makes bridle bits. Herrero is the name for blacksmith. If we had tools some of the young men could learn to make things; could learn very quick."

Thus spoke Herrero in 1865. He was and is still remembered, many years later, by his own people as Atsidi Sani (the Old Smith).

The Franciscan Fathers in their *Ethnologic Dictionary of the Navaho Language* mention him thus:

"According to the saying of some of the old silversmiths of the tribe, the art of working silver was introduced among them by the Mexicans about sixty years ago, or about the middle of the nineteenth century, when a Navaho blacksmith, known by his own people as *Atsidi Sani,* or 'the old smith,' and by the Mexicans as Herrero, or 'the smith,' first learned the art from a Mexican silversmith named Cassilio, who is said to have been still living in 1872–1873. An old silversmith, *Beshlagai ihl ini ahlts osigi,* or 'the slender silversmith,' who was still living (1909) and who at one time was considered one of the best, if not the best silversmith in the tribe, is said to have originally learned his craft from Mexicans. The Navaho silversmith, therefore, is a comparatively modern product."[25]

Once the road into the Navajo country was made comparatively safe for outsiders, there is little doubt that other Mexican smiths and traders soon invaded the area. It stands to reason that these *plateros* of a later date may have been responsible for the wider spread of the art, and by the 1880s,[26] when the American traders began to flourish, Mexican smiths were wandering through the territory making up silver ornaments and taking horses in exchange for their labor. In addition to these smiths, the native craftsmen were steadily pushing ahead until finally they had no further need of Mexican tutors and were self-sufficient in their craft.

It is significant to note, however, that the first observers of native smithing specifically mention the manufacture of buckles, buttons, and clasps of silver for the garments. No mention of bracelets, rings or *conchas.*

4: Ornament Forms

Their Origins

WHEN ONE ATTEMPTS a classification of the various forms of Navajo jewelry today, one is impressed by the tremendous array of bracelets, rings, pins, necklaces, belts, tie clasps, cigarette boxes, teaspoons, etc., fashioned into a thousand and one elaborate designs and set with turquoise of all colors and sizes.

However, basically, there were but few forms out of which this great family grew. There is no doubt that within past years the Navajo, prompted by the desires of traders and uninformed tourists, have originated certain patterns and styles which may be said to be their own brain children. The bulk of these rings and bracelets are over ornate, in some instances bordering on the grotesque and rococco.

The original forms of all the silverware manufactured by the Navajo were relatively simple; that is, those objects which spread from the Plains area to the Navajo country were made of thin, light metals, principally German silver, brass and copper. These were bracelets, rings, earrings, and belt *conchas*.

German silver, which is an alloy that contains no silver,[27] was a favored metal of the Plains tribes. The rings, bracelets, and hair plates, which in turn became belt *conchas,* worn by the Kiowa, Comanche, Dakota, Cheyenne, Ute, Pawnee, Osage, etc., were of this thin metal.

It was not until the Navajo began manufacturing their own ornaments that these various items began to appear in heavy coin silver.

Conchas

These *conchas* (shells), as they were known in New Mexico, were large, oval or circular, silver brooch-like ornaments which had been used extensively east of the Mississippi River as hair plates. These were of varying sizes and were worn in overlapping array hanging down the back fastened to a long lock of hair, hence the name.[28]

On the Plains, they continued to be used as hair ornaments, but like so many other bits of material culture, when transplanted they were adapted to other usages. From long locks of hair hanging down the back, it was but a short jump to long tapering straps of leather which were worn as belts or which hung down the sides of women's dresses suspended from the belts.[29]

The white traders and trappers, who penetrated the Rocky Mountains in the 1820s–1830s, did not encounter the Navajo but they did trade with the Ute, Kiowa, Comanche, Dakota, Crow, Cheyenne,[30] and other tribes of whom some were ancient enemies of the Navajo. The booty of a man slain in battle belonged to the man who slew him. The Navajo and the Ute were hereditary enemies.[31] The Comanche and the Kiowa also fought the Navajo. All of these people wore silver or German silver ornaments. Hence the acquisition of silver belts and silver mounted bridles by the Navajo was an easy matter.

On the other hand, some of the Mexican bridles had silver *conchas* on the head stalls. These were different in character from the belt *conchas* of the Plains, smaller and more elaborate in design. It is significant to note that the earliest Navajo belt *conchas* are large and quite simple in design. In fact some of them had no design. Others bore engraved patterns in light lines, or were scalloped around the edge. These were the identical patterns of the hair plates and belt *conchas* worn by the Plains Indian. The elaborate fluted and stamped *conchas* are a later development. Moreover, the older *conchas* are round, and so were those on the captured belts taken from the Ute, Comanche, etc. Hence, it would seem that while both oval and round *conchas* were used by the Plains people, the round predominated, and those were the first types copied by the Navajo when they learned to do their own smithing. The oval *conchas,* elaborately stamped and later set with turquoise, denoted the changing tastes and styles, far removed from the earlier forms.

When one examines the old *conchas* used by the Plains Indians one is impressed by the simplicity of design and this same simplicity was carried through to the first conchas manufactured by the Navajo. In fact the latter craftsmen simply copied the ones that fell into their hands.

A glance at the various types of *conchas* illustrated in Figure 1 will enable the reader to obtain a fair idea of the design elements embodied in the Plains prototypes, the Mexican bridle *conchas* and those made by the Navajo. Many of the earliest *conchas* fabricated by the Navajo were plain, slightly convex discs, with lightly scalloped edges. These scallops were filed, and the patterns, if any, were incised on the surface with a sharp pointed file. These are exact replicas of the contemporary

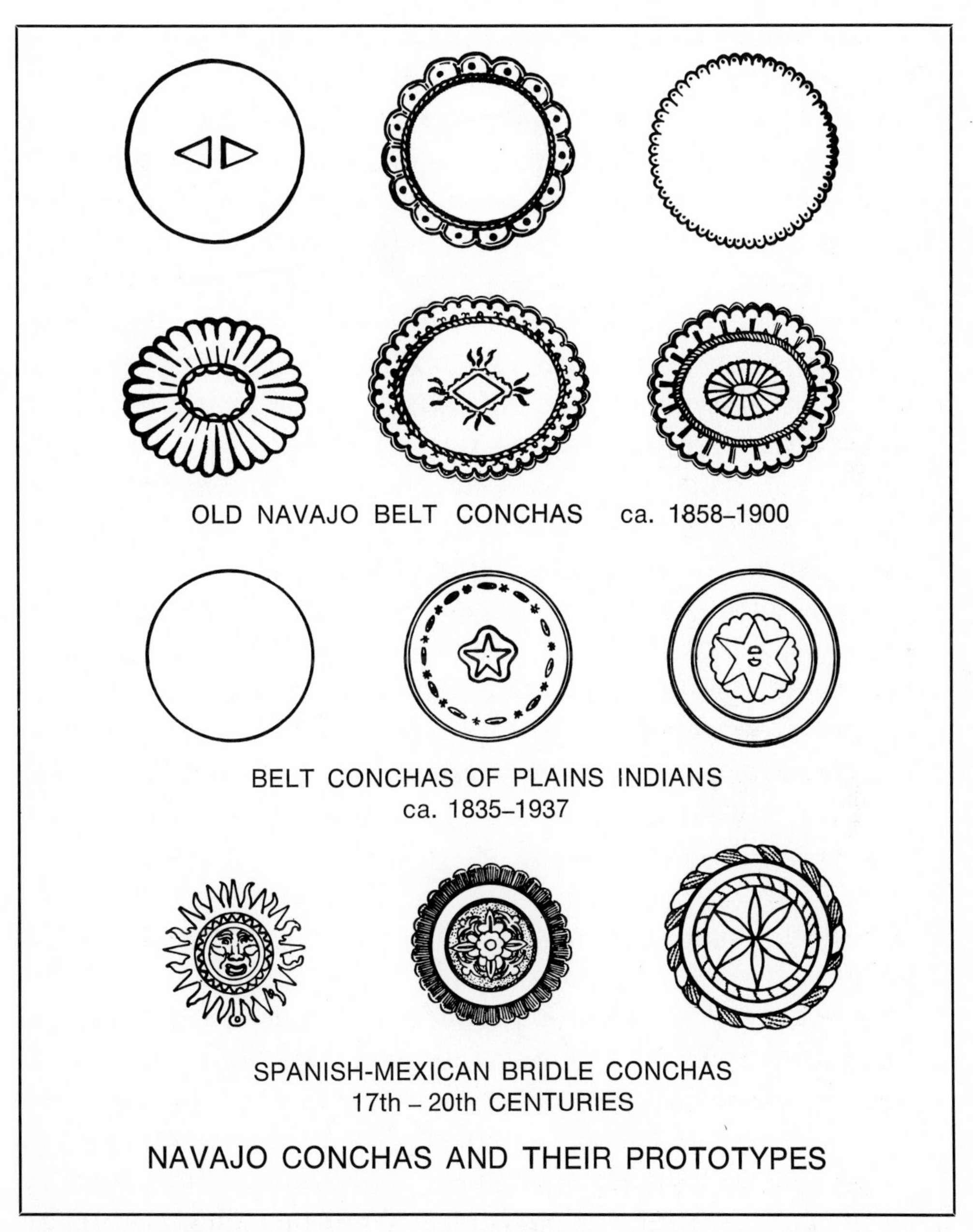

Figure 1. Patterns of belt and bridle *conchas* derived from original specimens and photographs. This plate is part of an exhibit of Navajo silverworking in the Los Angeles Museum.

Plains belt *conchas* and they in turn were modified patterns of the large brooches and hair plates used by the Eastern Indians.

Old Mexican bridle *conchas* are more elaborately chased, similar to the "sun" design shown on Figure 1. The use of floral and elaborate geometric patterns was also characteristic of the Mexican-Spanish *conchas,* and the latter were generally much smaller than the belt *conchas* made by the Navajo or worn by the Plains tribes.

Hence, when one considers the Indian decorative elements that have entered into the *conchas* made by the Navajo silversmiths, they are few and far between. The Navajo, not having worked in metal before, had no precedents for such designs; hence, they borrowed from the sources mentioned, and by combining and re-combining the various elements found in the Plains silver and Mexican leather, they evolved what has been termed true Navajo patterns (Fig. 2). As a matter of fact, those elements that crept in via the Plains route had originally been introduced by white silversmiths who decorated the silver trinkets for the Eastern Woodland people in the middle of the eighteenth century.

Bracelets

These ornaments are perhaps more common than any other product of th Navajo forge except finger-rings. I am not taking into account the numerous modern objects such as tie pins, pendants, cigarette boxes, trays, teaspoons, paper knives, tie clasps, etc. As a matter of fact I am not so concerned with the development of these latter items. They are modern symbols of present-day Navajo smithing to be sure, but they were not developed as a form of native ornament or utility, and reflect in most instances the peculiarly innate bad taste of the average American tourist who seemingly demands the gaudiest of gim-

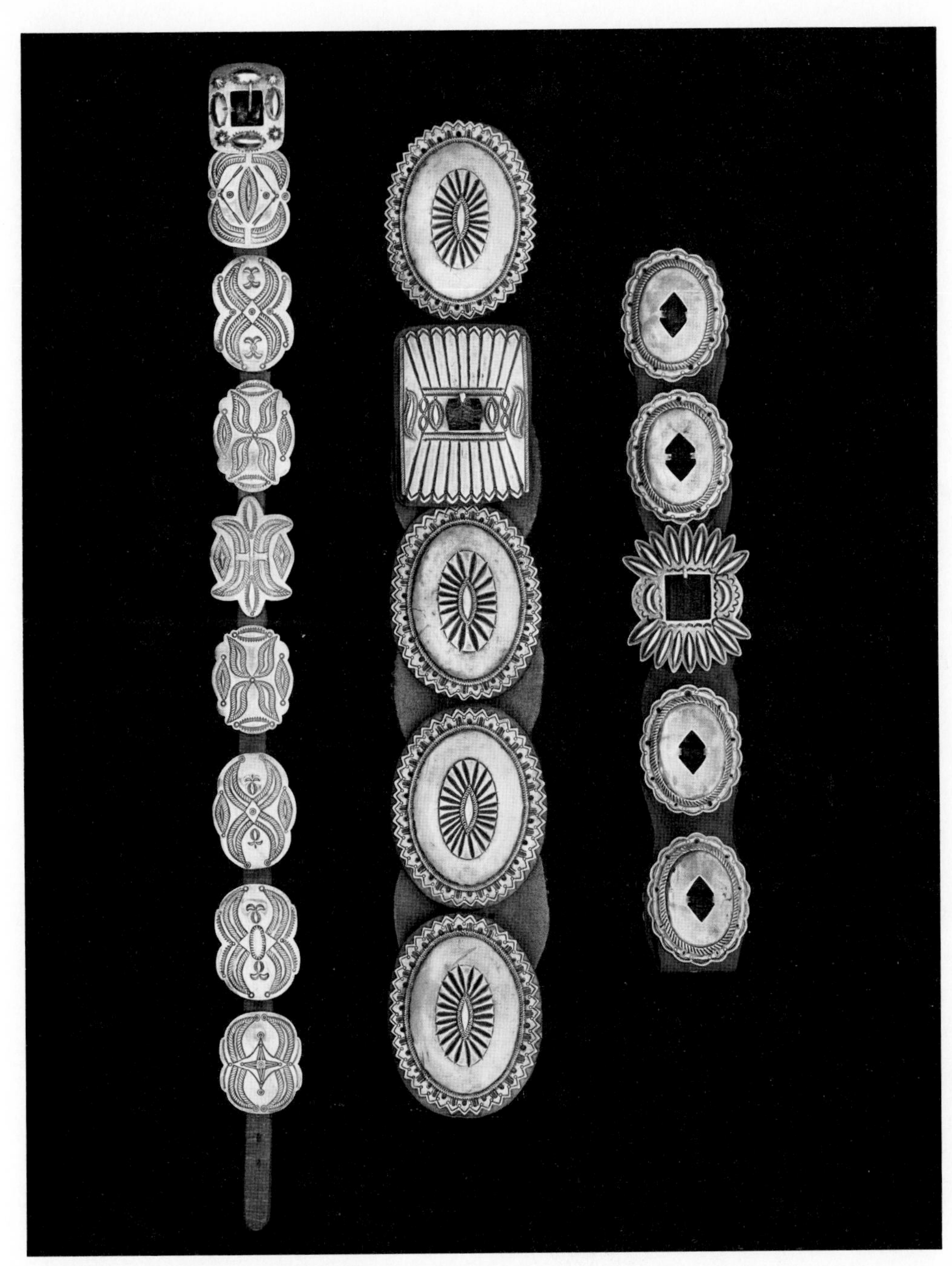

Figure 2. Navajo silver belts.

cracks when shopping away from home. Not that all of the modern bits of elaborately concocted creations of silver and turquoise are bad, far from it, but in the main they do not reflect the simple, normally well-conceived artistic jewelry of the natives themselves. It seems to be inevitable that whenever the American Indian has adopted some art or craft from the white man and has adapted it to aboriginal use, the white man in time takes back the contribution in the altered form and proceeds to spoil both the product and the artistry that created it. This holds true with weapons, utensils, costume, etc.

In considering the bracelets, one is immediately struck by the fact that the first ornaments of this class which came into the Navajo country from neighboring tribesmen to the north and east and which were copied by the Navajo when they began to manufacture their own ornaments, are the familiar types which were once seen upon the arms and wrists of the eastern Indians.

There were, in the beginning, a few essentially simple patterns. From these armlets evolved the thousands of bracelets now known as Navajo wares. Virtually every one of these bracelet forms has its exact or nearly exact counterpart among the ornaments worn by the Iroquois, Cherokee, Yuchi, Delaware, and Upper Plains people. This statement applies not only to the forms but to the designs engraved or stamped upon the surface.

Few of the earliest bracelets were of heavy silver. They were thin, flattened strips of hammered or sheet metal, and the designs were scratched or engraved upon the metal with some sharp pointed steel tool.

These flat bracelets were of varying widths. East of the Mississippi the wide arm bands worn above the elbow were popular, but these armlets failed to obtain a foothold in the Navajo country. On the other hand the narrow, plain or engraved

Figure 3. Navajo bracelets. Simple stamped patterns.

flat bracelets or wrist bands were eagerly accepted. As one examines the bracelets of this type worn by the Iroquois and the Dakota, one is immediately impressed with the nature of the designs. Those which were originally manufactured by the white silversmiths are naturally more finished in technique, particularly the patterns inscribed with an engraving tool, and few of the eighteenth century and early nineteenth century ornaments supplied to the Indian trade bore the stamped patterns of a few decades later. The German silver bracelets of the early 1830s begin to show the more mechanical, repeated patterns produced by stamping. However, even in these cases, the design elements, repeated, are virtually the same as those of the earlier periods.

We know that when the Iroquois, Cherokee, and Delaware native smiths began plying their trade in the nineteenth century, they used stamps and dies made out of pieces of scrap iron.[32] Subsequently their Navajo brethren did the same thing. However, the patterns as adopted by the Navajo are somewhat different and for this reason: the Navajo dies were apparently those used in tooling Mexican leatherwork. I have examined eighteenth and early nineteenth century Mexican leatherwork, saddles, saddle skirts, *botas* (leggings), chair and bench coverings, leather covered chests, knife and sword scabbards, etc., and have noticed the identical designs used on Navajo jewelry. Those same patterns persist to this day (Fig. 3). Hence, to attempt a translation of the meaning of these varied design elements in terms of native symbols is but to rationalize. I do not say that the Navajo craftsmen have not combined these same elements in designs of their own. They have, but I do maintain that the original elements of the die patterns were not native in concept and cannot logically be so interpreted.

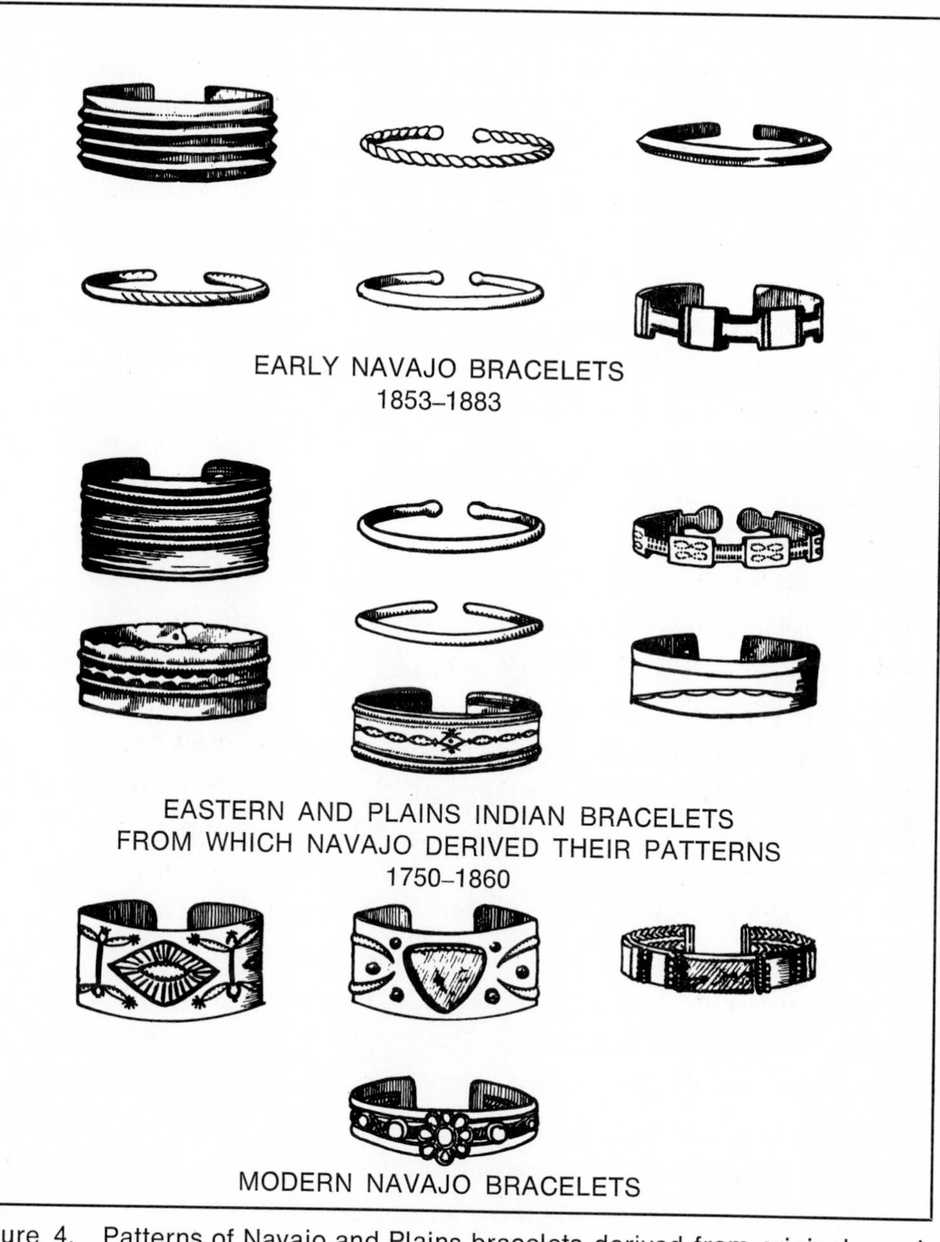

Figure 4. Patterns of Navajo and Plains bracelets derived from original specimens and illustrations. Note the similarity between the early Navajo forms and those used on the Plains and in the East. This plate is part of an exhibit of Navajo silverworking in the Los Angeles Museum.

Ridged or Fluted Bracelets

These were popular in the Iroquois country one hundred years before the Navajo began making them. Originally they were made in brass and copper. The Dakota, Utes, and other Plains tribes also wore these non-precious ornaments. It is a significant fact that during the 1830s and 1840s when the Plains and Rocky Mountain tribes were obtaining the bulk of their cheap jewelry from white traders, these broad, fluted wrist bands were in their heyday, and it was during this same period that the Navajo also began to obtain these same ornaments, in a secondary fashion through trade or spoils of war.

On Figure 4 I have indicated the comparative types of bracelets, and it will be noted that the ridged types have changed but little. In recent years there has been a strong revival of this pattern, mainly through the desire of traders and students to revive old styles. However, the later bracelets have heavier, sharper ridges than the earlier ones, a change brought about by the individual workmanship of the modern smiths. These fluted wrist bands are the broadest of all the bracelets, although some of the stamped flat bands equal them in width at times.

Twisted Bracelets

Under this heading may be designated those simple ornaments which are made of single strands of heavy twisted silver wire. In turn, these single strands are often doubled or trebled by the Navajo to form pleasing bracelets which are frequently set with turquoise of varying sizes.

The earliest of these bracelets were of brass, copper, or iron wire and were worn singly or by the half dozen on the wrist. Coexistent with these twisted wire forms were the single strands of brass or iron wire, clipped and bent around the arm thus forming the most common style of armlet. These too, had their inception east of the Mississippi and spread west with the ebbing tide of trade.

It has been stated that the Navajo began making most of this style ornament during and immediately after their incarceration in Bosque Redondo, but they were wearing them before this period, and I am satisfied that such ornaments were those that were taken in such quantities to the western country by the American fur traders.

Rings

The first rings obtained by the Navajo were the same as those worn on the Plains. In turn these cheap brass or German silver finger adornments were patterned after those issued to the Eastern tribes. The long, oval bezel of plain or etched silver was a favorite among the Iroquois and Delaware. It found ready favor among the Dakota. The Navajo adopted it. Rings having square bezels or none at all were likewise favored. The early rings used east of the Mississippi were in brass and then of good coin silver. On the Plains they were brass or German silver. Rings of the two latter metals reached the Navajo via the familiar Plains route which led through the Ute country. In turn these basic forms laid the foundations for the turquoise settings which are so popular at the present time. As a matter of fact, during the first sixty years of the nineteenth century, the trade rings were frequently set with colored glass. The native-made silver rings of the Iroquois were also set with glass. Although it has been deemed that the Navajo did not begin to use turquoise, garnets, glass, etc., prior to about 1900, Mrs. Matilda C. Stevenson wrote that:

"The first setting of turquoise in silver occurred about 1880. It was done by a Navaho in a ring which he presented to the writer."[33]

Oddly enough, the method of setting the first turquoise in

rings, by Navajo smiths, was the same as that used in the setting of glass paste jewels in the trade jewelry sold by white traders to the various tribesmen during the first half of the nineteenth century, namely by the use of a series of tiny triangular prongs which gave a rather pleasing effect to the surface of the inset.

The patterns engraved upon the flat surfaces of the oval and rectangular bezels of the early Navajo rings were also the same as those found upon the Plains trade jewelry.

Earrings

The original form of the earrings made in silver were relatively few in number and simple in workmanship. They varied from plain, unadorned circlets of silver or brass wire, with or without hollow silver beads fastened to them, to crescent shaped pieces of silver with hinged center sections, and long "tear drops" terminating in small silver pomegranates. Others were circles of silver wire partially flattened and either engraved or stamped with simple patterns. With the possible exception of the "tear drop" ear ornaments, practically every one of these early styles was in vogue among the Indians east of the Mississippi. The crescent shaped earrings with the hinged sections were popular among the Shawnee and Delaware. On Figure 5 are depicted some of these early forms, including one of the elongated ear drops. (See also Fig. 13.) This latter ornament seems to be a Mexican cape ornament adopted without change. During the eighteenth and early nineteenth centuries these ornaments, fashioned of gold and silver in this precise form, decorated the broadcloth and velvet capes worn by the better class Mexicans. Excellent samples of these objects, still fastened to the original garment, may be seen in the Sepulveda collection of Spanish-Californian costumes at the Bowers Memorial Museum, Santa Ana, California. An excellent pair of earrings of this type is in

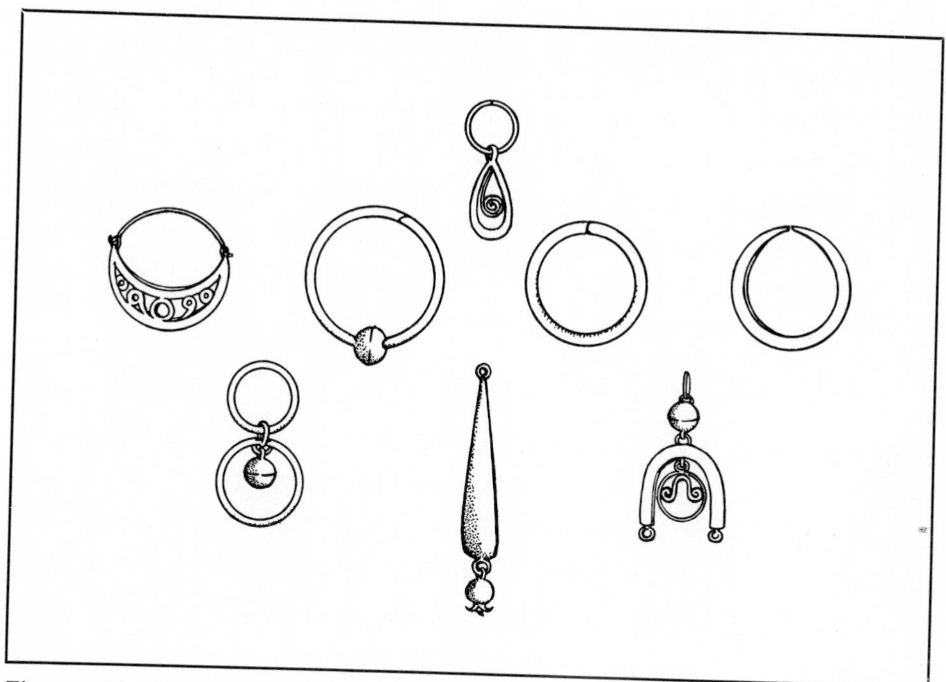

Figure 5. Sketches of Navajo earrings. (After Lummis, 1896.)

the collection of the Southwest Museum, Los Angeles. The line drawing is after Lummis. (See Bibliography.)

Buttons

When we consider the various types of buttons employed by the Navajos in decorating their garments we invade the sphere of Hispano-Mexican influences and leave the Eastern field.

The Mexicans of the eighteenth-nineteenth centuries were lavish in the use of silver and gold buttons on their garments as I have already indicated. These fasteners were of many shapes and sizes. Some were flat, without any design. Others were round, dome-shaped, conical (Fig. 13), or fashioned to represent pomegranates. Some were decorated with punched designs or fluted with straight lines (Figs. 6 and 7). We find the Navajo using every single one of these types and generally in the same

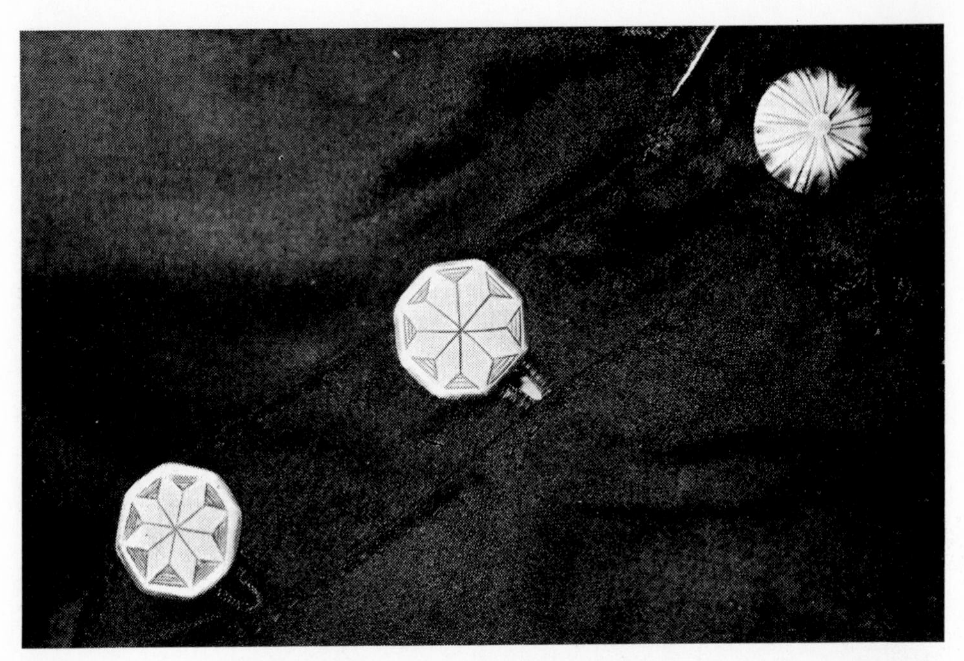

Figure 6. Mexican-Californian silver trouser buttons. Note similarity between the dome shaped button in this illustration and buttons in Figure 7. Del Valle Collection, Los Angeles Museum.

manner in which they were first employed by the Mexicans.

On the other hand, certain forms of these buttons were adapted by the Indians for other purposes which will be discussed in the section devoted to necklaces.

And, even as the Iroquois women of the eighteenth century were prone to use the silver brooches that covered their shifts and leggings, row on row, as currency in the trading posts,[34] so do their Navajo sisters use their buttons today. In the Navajo country at the present time one notes many American quarters, dimes, and half dollars with small copper loops soldered on one side doing double duty as buttons and the family small cash supply. The same system of accepting Indian silver ornaments as pawn prevailed among the eighteenth century Indian trad-

Figure 7. Navajo silver buttons.

ers as it does today among the American traders on the Navajo reservation.

Necklaces

The heavy silver necklaces worn by the Navajo are composed of round, ovoid, or so-called "squash blossom" beads (Fig. 8).

It is my contention that all of these beads were originally Spanish-Mexican trouser and jacket ornaments. I have previously mentioned the extensive use of silver ball buttons and those which were fashioned to resemble the pomegranate.

The latter fruit has been a favorite Spanish decorative motif for centuries. It is found on the Spanish coat-of-arms representing the city of Granada, which of course means "pomegranate." It was used extensively as an ecclesiastical decoration. One observes it painted upon the ruined ceiling of the old Cocospera mission in Sonora, and the ceiling under the choir loft in the Franciscan church of Tubutama in the same state, was stuck full of carved and gilded pomegranates until the acquisitive tourist depleted the supply.

In Figure 9 are shown the silver pomegranates dangling from short silver chains on a pair of Mexican-Californian trousers, ca. 1834–1840, now in the Los Angeles Museum.

The Navajo silver ornaments of this type, seen so extensively on necklaces, have been referred to, without any adequate basis for so doing, other than rationalism, as "squash blossoms," or "sun flower blossoms." With so many examples of this type ornament in existence on Mexican costumes, either trousers, jackets, or capes, it seems foolish to look farther afield for the prototypes of this highly popular necklace element. If one were to remove these buttons or cape ornaments from the original garments and string them, the result would be a fine "old" Navajo necklace. In Figure 10 I have illustrated side by side a sketch of a young pomegranate, a Mexican trouser ornament, and a bead from a Navajo necklace.

Naja or Crescent

Hanging pendant from any good Navajo necklace may usually be seen a rather heavy, cast, single or double crescent, the tips of which generally terminate in small round buttons or tiny hands (Fig. 8). Sometimes these tips are joined (Fig. 11).

Attention has been called time and again, more recently by Miss Bedinger (1936), to this ornament. However, she is uncertain as to whether it may not have originated with the Navajo and she speaks of it as a "true Navajo concept." She further speaks of "The variety among *najas* gives ample proof of the virility of the design sense of the Navajo. Although they always conform to the rigid conventions, yet by varying the proportions

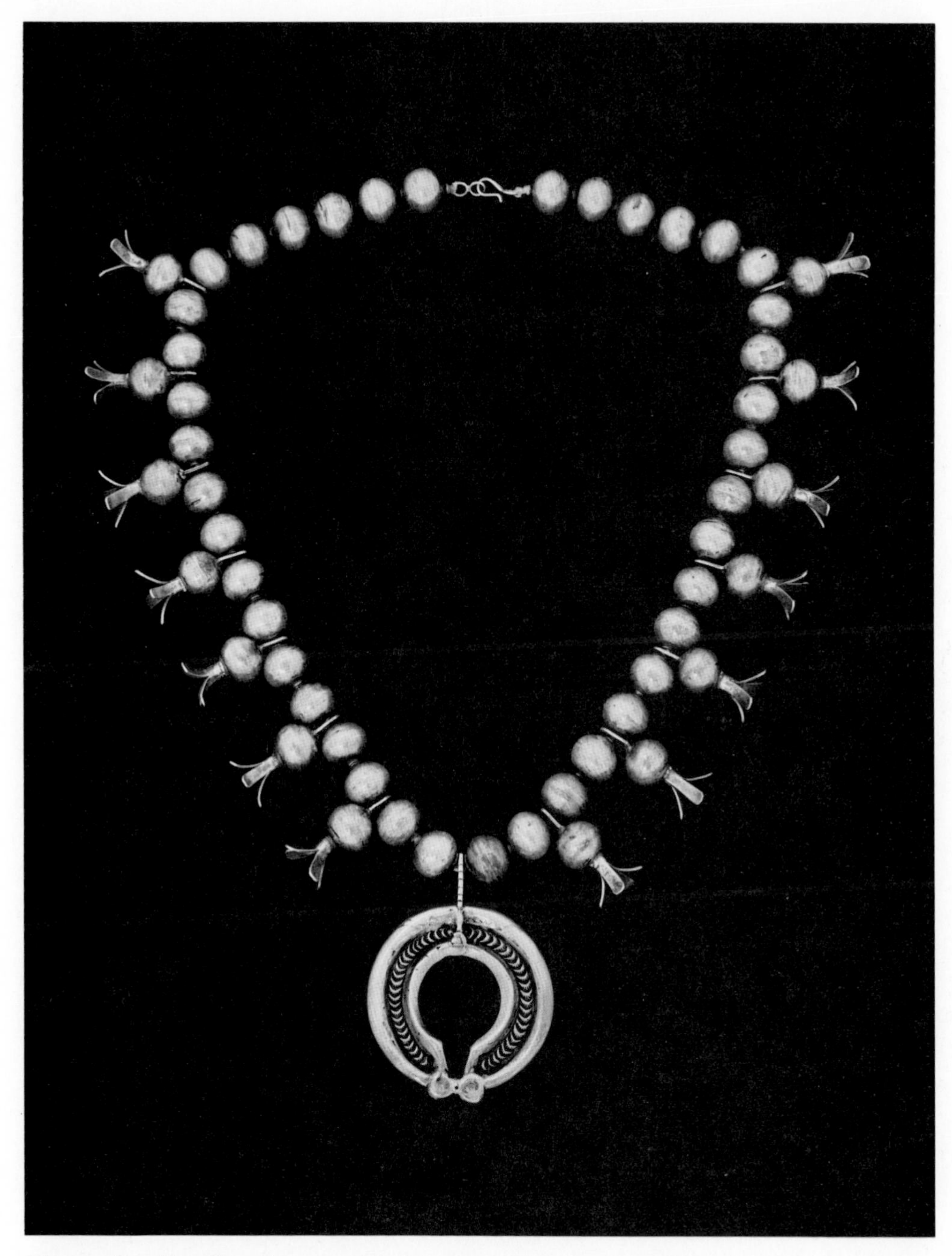

Figure 8. Navajo silver necklace, "pomegranate" pattern.

Figure 9. Silver clasps and pomegranate ornaments on pair of original Mexican-Californian trousers, ca. 1834–1840. The Coronel Collection, Los Angeles Museum.

and the curve of the crescent, by the use of turquoise [Fig. 13], by the decoration of the arms, an endless difference of beauty is obtained to the continual delight of the lover of this art. For instance, in one unusual old one, the curved arms end in tiny hands instead of the common buttons. In some of the older *najas* the circle is closed."[35]

Again, she quotes the words of a Navajo, Long Mustache, regarding the manufacture of silver bridles by the Navajo. . . . "After they had learned to make belts the Navajos made silver-mounted headstalls for their bridles [Fig. 12]. These consisted of a center-piece nicely decorated, from which hung a moon-like crescent, like a horse shoe. . . ."

Here, in this last statement is actually the whole crux of the matter. The *naja* in its varying forms from open to closed circle, small rounded buttons, hands, and dangling center pendant, is

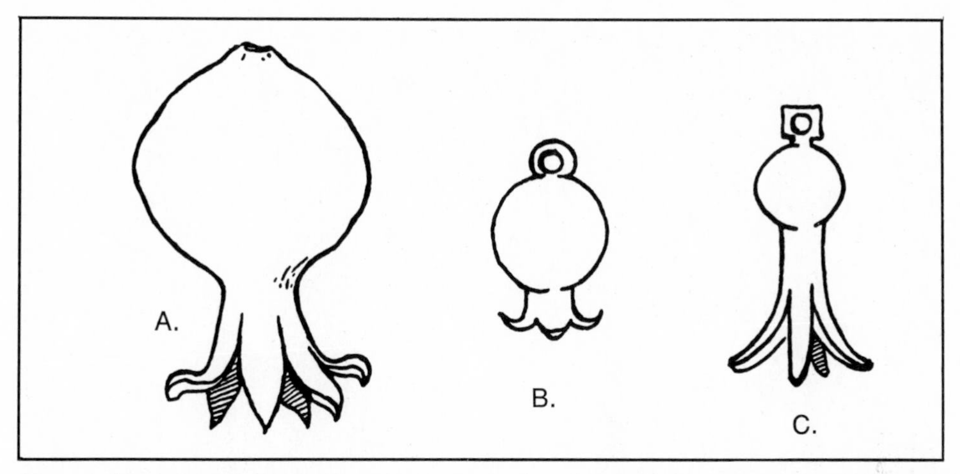

Figure 10. A. A young pomegranate; B. A Mexican trouser ornament; C. Navajo squash blossom.

not Navajo in concept. This emblem was old when Columbus crossed the ocean to the new world. It was wide spread from Africa to Serbia. In short, it was an Old World amulet fastened to horse trappings, preferably the bridle, to ward off the evil eye from the animal. These crescent-shaped amulets were made of two boar tusks joined together or fashioned out of brass, iron, silver, gold, or bronze. The Romans had them, so did the Moors.[36] The bridle trappings of the *conquistadores* no doubt carried these same traditional ornaments.

Other Indian tribes were using silver plated bridles as early or earlier than the Navajo. German silver adorned the Kiowa-Comanche horse trappings during the early decades of the eighteenth century.[37] Those bridles bore the crescent-shaped ornaments, and in time the same crescent forms were also used as earrings. Hence there seems a good chance that the Navajo obtained the *naja* from bridles in silver or brass or German silver from the Kiowa-Comanche area; or the Ute, who were traditional enemies of both the Kiowa and the Navajo, received it from the Kiowa and transmitted it to the Navajo. In my mind

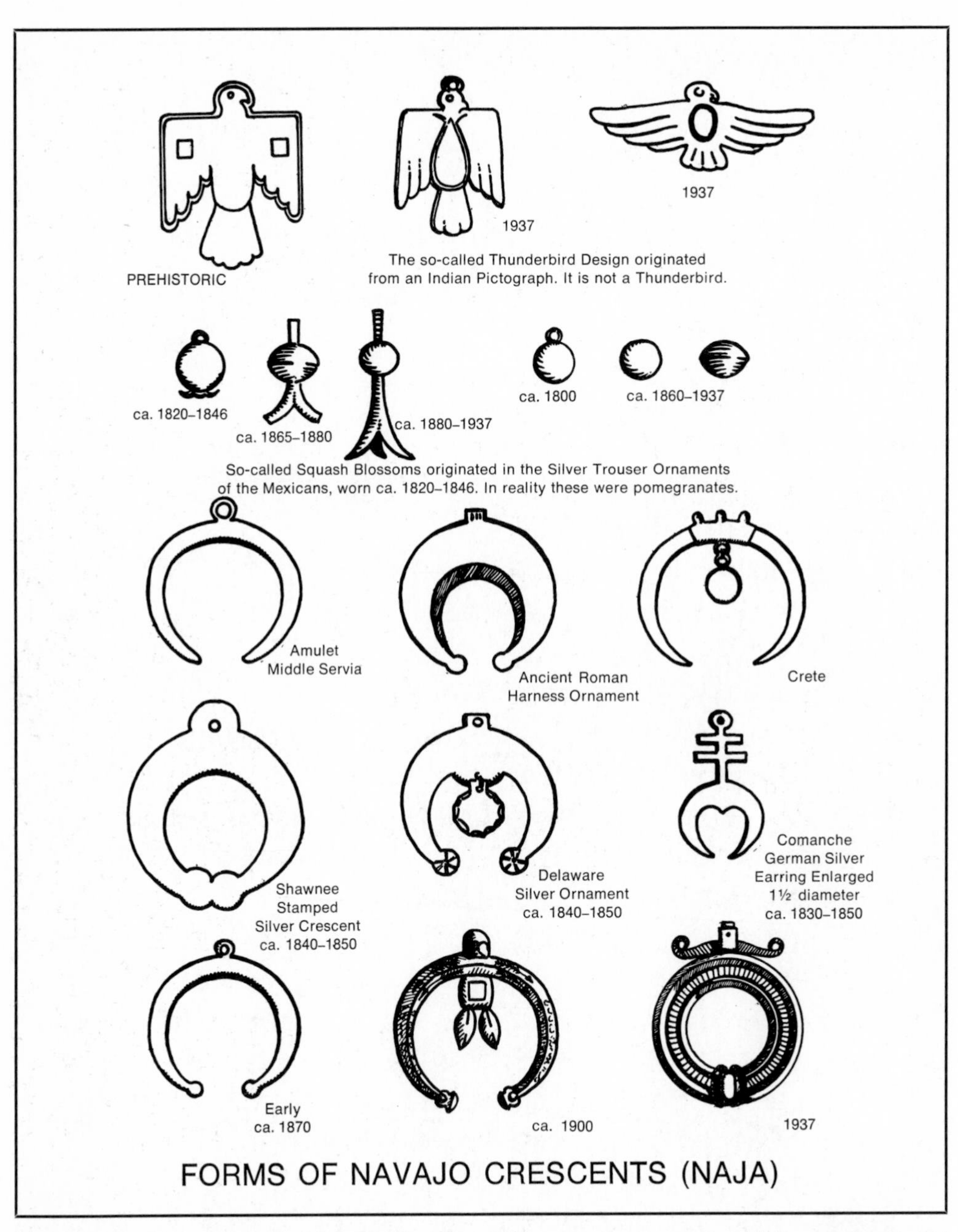

Figure 11. Illustrating various forms of Navajo ornaments. Note ancient and modern types of the *naja.* This plate is part of an exhibit on Navajo silverworking in the Los Angeles Museum.

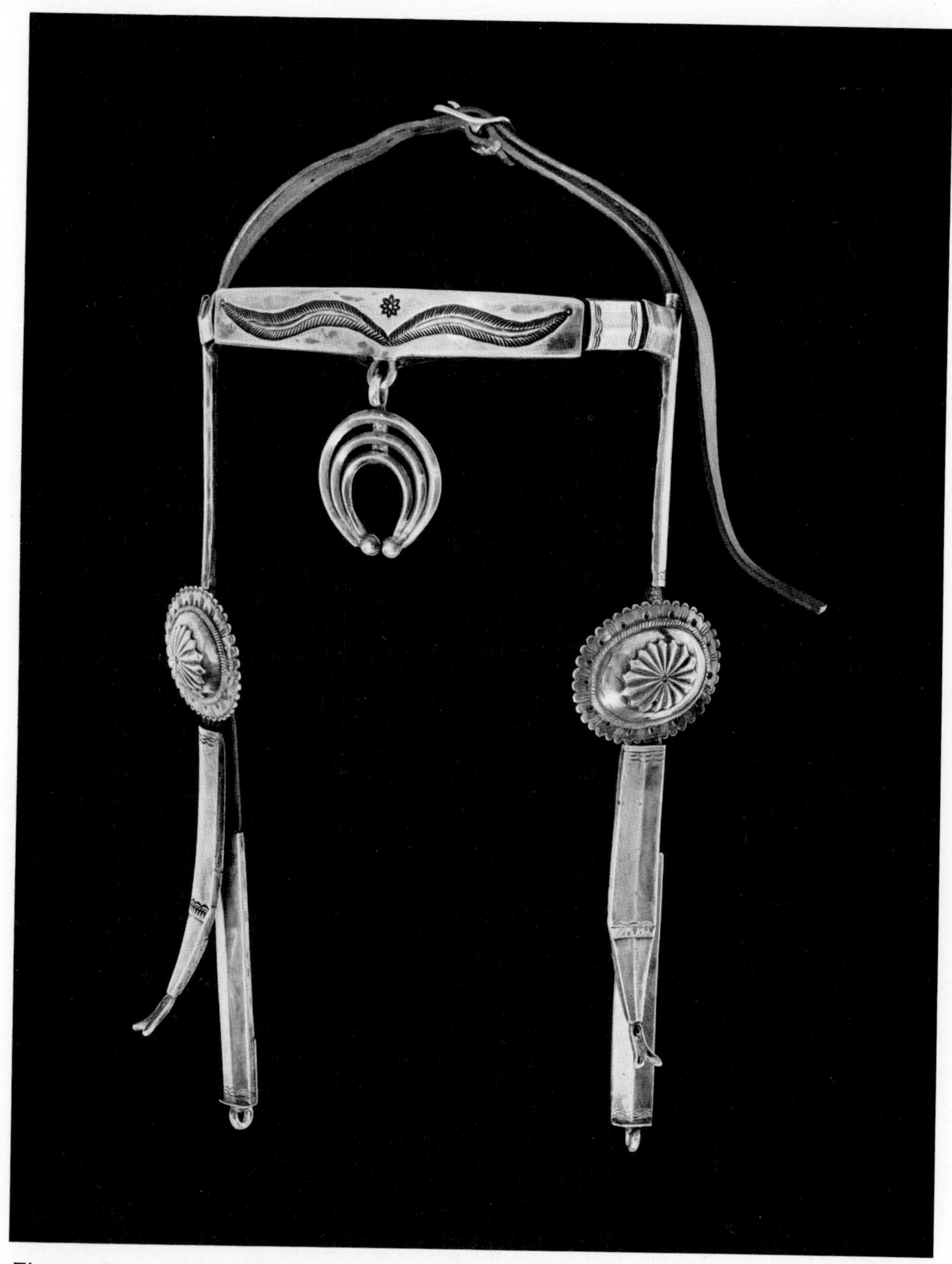

Figure 12. Silver mounted Navajo bridle.

this seems a more logical course. Moreover, the Delaware, who moved into the Oklahoma country early in the nineteenth century, were silversmiths, having carried the trade with them from east of the Mississippi. The first native ornaments *made* in the southern Plains were the products of Delaware smiths. The latter in turn taught the art to the Kiowa who practice it today. On Figure 11 are shown two early *najas*, collected among the Delaware and Shawnee of Oklahoma, now in the Museum of the American Indian. These are old specimens and are of rather thin stamped or hammered silver, and correspond to the early forms of this ornament rather than the later heavier ones made by the Navajo. It will be noted that the Shawnee specimen is joined together at the tips of the crescent. The Delaware item terminates in vestigal hands and bears a swinging bangle in the center of the inner curve of the ornament. A similar thin *naja* is in the collections of the National Museum. However, it resembles the one from the Shawnee country rather than the Delaware, but this is of little import since the Delaware and Shawnee people were closely allied during the last half of the eighteenth century and the types of silver ornaments used by those tribes were virtually the same.

It has always seemed to me that *if* the Navajo had obtained the bulk of their silver mounted bridles directly from the Spanish, instead of through the avenues mentioned, their presence would have been noted much earlier.

The average Spaniard or Mexican used his silver covered horse gear on special occasions, such as weddings, fiestas, etc., and seldom on a campaign. Hence, the opportunity for capture of such items from the Spanish would be rare compared to the chances of taking them in battle with the Ute or Kiowa. Miss Bedinger's informant specifically states the Ute were the first Indians to have bridles like these.[38] As I have indicated, this is not wholly true. Hence we may conclude that the *naja* came to the Navajo in its various forms from the bridles used by the Ute *and* the Kiowa, and those same *najas* were identical in form with those first used centuries ago in Europe to ward off the evil eye from horses.

Miscellaneous

Among the most familiar pendants and pins manufactured within recent years by Navajo smiths are those representing a bird with outspread wings. This ornament is widely known as the "Thunderbird," in spite of the fact that the "Thunderbird" is an unknown factor in the mythology of the Southwest.

On the other hand the bird figure is commonly seen in prehistoric pictographs, on ancient and modern pottery, and is prevalent in the mythology of the Puebloan and Navajo tribes.

The current story connected with the so-called "Thunderbird" pattern is that this particular design was first noted by surveyors for the Santa Fe railroad near Scholle, New Mexico. The discovery of a number of beautifully executed pictographs in polychrome was relayed to the office in Albuquerque and copies were made of the various figures.

The bird figure was ultimately adopted by the railroad as a trademark and in turn the curio shops along the line began selling silver replicas of this bird. It was termed a "Thunderbird" mainly through ignorance.

Whether this story is true I cannot say, but I can vouch for the fact that the prehistoric pictograph of this particular bird form painted in blue-gray and white does appear in conjunction with numerous other finely executed figures, on overhanging rocks alongside the road to Abó, not far from Scholle. I visited this spot in company with Mr. Frank Pinkley, Superintendent of Southwestern Monuments, National Park Service, in November, 1935, and made sketches of some of the figures (Fig. 11).

Old forms of Navajo silverwork no longer seen include the small round canteens, souvenirs made for the soldiers at Fort Defiance in the 1870s and 1880s, replicas of the water containers carried by the troopers. Powder chargers, such as those illustrated by Matthews,[39] fashioned in the shape of arrows, are likewise things of the past. Time was when nearly every man who owned a muzzle-loading gun used a powder charger with which he measured out the precise amount of powder needed for his weapon. Uusually these were cut out of wood, deer antler or cow horn. The silver chargers made by the Navajo were no doubt patterned on those they had first seen used by the Mexicans and Americans. The silver chains attached to the chargers were likewise a complement of the regular ones; either a chain or a cord was used to fasten the charger to the shoulder strap from which hung the shot pouch and powder horn.

In recent years thin bands of stamped silver have appeared on the hats of Navajo men. It is odd that these modern native smiths should begin to manufacture such objects, which in form at least are the same as those silver hat and head bands manufactured by the Iroquois smiths a half century before the Navajo began working in silver.

However, in this instance I do not believe the Eastern Indian prototypes had any bearing upon the Navajo wares. As Miss Bedinger has pointed out, these probably originated in the beaded or horsehair hat bands which came to the Southwest from Mexican and Plains Indian sources. As far as I am aware the silver head bands of the East and South did not penetrate the Plains, mainly for the reason that the headgear of the latter area was entirely different from that of the former region.

During the latter part of the eighteenth and past the middle of the nineteenth century, thin silver head bands, worn over

Figure 13. Navajo ornaments. Buttons, *naja* with a turquoise, and earrings.

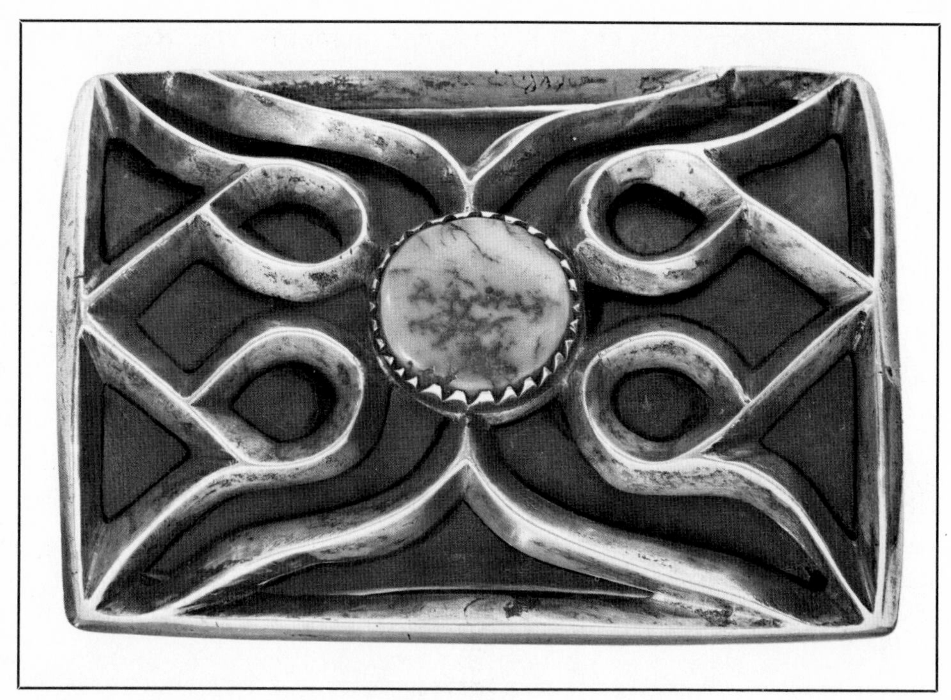

Figure 14. Navajo *Keto* or bow guard, of cast silver.

turbans and later, the high beaver hats, were in vogue among the Iroquois, Ottawa, Delaware, Cherokee, Creek, Alibamu, etc. These bands were both plain and ornamented, some of the latter being quite elaborately engraved and perforated and hung with little bangles.

Delaware Indian scouts serving with the Union army during the Civil War wore a curious combination of military and tribal costume. Some of these were quite fantastic and not the least incongruous were the long peacock feathers fastened to their hats which in turn were adorned with wide silver bands.[40]

The *keto,* Bow Guard, Wristlet or Bracer: In discussing the various ornament forms I purposely avoided mentioning the *keto* or bow guard (Fig. 14). Although I have some ideas concerning its origin I have but one reference that confirms this suspicion. My feeling is that the metal covered leather bracer developed from the broad brass wristlets used by the Utes. Then the thin brass and copper were cut into plates and fastened to the leather. From this it was but a simple step to the use of silver in place of the baser metals. In describing the costume of the Ute (which the author mistook for Navajo) Furber (1850, p. 255) said: "In addition to the dress mentioned, all wore bracelets of brass upon their wrists, to protect this part from the string of the bow when shooting an arrow."

In primitive times I believe the Navajo in common with other tribesmen used leather bracers to protect their wrists from the bow string. When metals began to be used it was a simple matter to overlay the leather and thus the various forms of the *keto* came into existence.

Use of Turquoise

Any discussion of the history of Navajo silversmithing would be incomplete without some reference to the use of turquoise by the native smiths. This section will deal mainly with a brief review of the stone as it is used today by the Navajo jewelers.

Turquoise has been a highly prized stone among the Indians of the Southwest for centuries. Long before the art of silver-working was introduced among the Navajo, this blue gem stone was fashioned into beads, earrings, and mosaics by the Puebloan tribes and by the peoples of Old Mexico.

The Navajo were making earrings of turquoise long before they began setting the stone in silver. In Mexico this mineral was worked into beautiful mosaics. The Aztecs termed it *chalchihuites,*which word was also applied to jadeite.

Mr. Sam Yost, editor of the *Santa Fe Weekly Gazette* and special agent to the Navajo, wrote to his paper from Fort Defiance on September 29, 1858, concerning the state of the

Navajo war and in describing some of the natural wonders of the country said:

"Specimens of stone or agate of the most variant and beautiful colors, are found in many places. Chalquiguithe, a bluish green stone, something after the turquoise, is found, very rarely however, and is valued higher than anything else by the Indians. Earrings made out of it are worth in their estimation, $100 and upwards. None but the *ricos* can afford to wear it.

"It is said Montezuma sent three pieces of this stone to Cortez as the most precious and valuable present that could be offered. It is found, I believe, somewhere near Zuñi. There is also an immense excavation twenty miles from Santa Fe, 200 feet wide and 300 feet deep, which it is supposed at one time was made to produce this precious stone. This, however, must have been made many years ago, as pine thickets have grown up at the bottom of the earthy aperture."

The *chalchihuite* to which Editor Yost referred in this instance was jadeite, the stone so prized by the ancient Mexicans. The quarry which he described was the well-known turquoise workings near Santa Fe, known as Los Cerrillos.

Today the bulk of the turquoise supplied to the Indian market in Arizona and New Mexico is derived from a number of mines in Nevada. Between 3,000 and 5,000 pounds of the blue stone are mined and shipped from Nevada each year, approximately 80 percent of the output going into the Indian country.

Among the better-known mines supplying this trade are:

Lone Mountain, sixteen miles west of Tonopah.

Blue Gem, forty miles north of Tonopah.

Black Matrix, near Carlin. This mine is famous for the fine black lines webbing the clear blue of the gem stone.

No. 8 (no definite name), also near Carlin.

Monitor Valley, one hundred five miles northeast of Tonopah.

Crow Springs, forty miles northwest of Tonopah.

Royal Blue, thirty miles north of Tonopah.

Cortez. The latter mine supplies much of the bead turquoise. However, it is said to be less desirable in color but easily worked, which makes it a favorite material for the cheaper grade of Indian necklaces.

From the Mineral Park Mines, Arizona, situated in Mohave County, twenty miles north from Kingman, is obtained a soft grade of greenish-hued turquoise.

Turquoise is graded according to color, marking of the matrix, and hardness. The best grades range from 6 in hardness to 3 in softness and in color through all variations from white, green, and blue. The hard blue stone is the best and is valued accordingly by the Indians who invest their money in it. The fine spiderweb Black Matrix is an excellent grade and the best stone from this mine is obtained at the eighty-five foot level.

The blue stone is sold by the carat. After the stones have been cut they sell at from ten to fifty cents per carat wholesale and will retail for twice that amount. Uncut or rough turquoise sells from $2.50 to $25 per pound. Bead turquoise is sold wholesale.

In preparing the turquoise for market the lapidary inspects his pieces of matrix and decides upon the most economical method of cutting the stone to obtain the most gems out of it. Once the stones have been cut, which is done by chipping away all of the surplus matrix (this is done at the mine), the next step is to place the turquoise on a carborundum stone. The latter abrasive is used almost exclusively in the turquoise grinding trade, the carborundum ranging from 80 coarse through 120 medium to 220 fine. Upon these varying grades of power-driven abrasive wheels the turquoise gems are cut to proper shapes.

This preliminary cutting leaves the stones dull and lifeless, or at best with a soft clean surface, and in this first stage they greatly resemble the finished product turned out by the native Indian workmen on their sandstone rubbing slabs used in reducing the matrix at home.

After the stones have been ground on the wheels they are gone over with fine carborundum cloth to remove the scratches that might have been left by the grinding.

The final stage of the polishing is done by cementing, with sealing wax, the cut stones on the end of pontil sticks, made of the ordinary wooden meat skewers used in butcher shops. By this method the gems are held against a buckskin buffing wheel coated with oxide of tin. This imparts a high gloss to the turquoise which is so characteristic of all lapidary cut stones. The native cut stones lack this polish and are easily recognized.

Although the best grade of turquoise is said to come from the Black Matrix Mine, the gem dealers report that the Indians prefer the stones taken from the Lone Mountain Mine, which run to a purer, cleaner grade with less matrix.

There are tricks to all trades and the modern turquoise vendors (except for the more reputable, who fortunately for the buying public are in the majority and do not engage in the practice) have a habit of dyeing the softer grades of stones to impart a greenish-blue color to them. The bulk of this dyeing has been done in Germany in recent years. The soft, white grades of turquoise are shipped to Germany where they are cut and dyed, the resultant stones being largely used as costume beads, and as settings in the cheaper jewelry manufactured in great quantities in Los Angeles, Denver, Albuquerque, and Santa Fe. This thin, cheaply made, over-ornate jewelry made with thin sheet metal and stereotyped dies was formerly advertised as being "Indian made." In a sense this was true because the wholesale manufacturers of such trash, particularly those in Albuquerque, hired young Navajo and Pueblo boys to operate the machinery necessary for its manufacture. I counted about forty such operators in one shop. It is now under the Federal Trade Commission ban. Its sale should be condemned by every honest curio dealer in the country.

In recent years, so I am informed, Oriental curio manufacturers have placed show cases filled with the cheap imitation Indian jewelry in some of the smaller stores in Los Angeles. Every month or so they check up on the sales of this spurious stuff, pay the dealers commissions on the items sold and restock the cases. I have seen hundreds of these fake rings, bracelets, and pins for sale in reputable department stores. However, the average buyer is not in a position to know this shoddy trash from the genuine Indian product, hence the dealers are able to continue this wholesale duping of the gullible public. The same Orientals are also selling small wood and bone "totem poles" and kachina dolls, not as Indian made, but the wording of their advertisements is such as to lead the buyers to think they are purchasing Indian souvenirs. All such trash is usually done in "Indian style." *Caveat emptor!*

The cutting of the small stones abroad is done chiefly in Oberstein, Germany where cheap labor makes it possible for the poor grade turquoise to be cut, dyed, polished, and sent back to this country where it is sold at a reasonable profit. Odd isn't it to think that the Navajo rings may be set with small turquoises that have journeyed to Germany and back to be vended by the Indian traders to tourists.

The dyeing of low grade turquoise is not confined to the Germans however. Unscrupulous American dealers, and perhaps some of the Indians who have the cheap, light-colored stones, have discovered that if the turquoise is boiled for two or three hours in mutton tallow, bacon drippings, lubricating oil, or paraffine, a variety of greenish tints are imparted to the soft matrix, giving the stones the appearance of having been worn some time.

These dyed turquoises are usually seen in graduated necklaces and are almost olive green in color. Now and then one sees old turquoise necklaces, earrings, settings in bracelets, or necklaces that are actually green with age, having absorbed a certain amount of grease through long contact with the wearer's skin. However, such stones are usually poor grade to begin with. Fine hard turquoise of clear blue seldom changes color.

One can detect the oil dyed stones by either smelling them or holding them in the hand for a few moments. In either case the odor of the oil is apparent, or in the latter instance the heat of the hand causes the oil to ooze from the stone and stick to the hand. In a Tucson shop, I once saw a matched strand of dyed turquoise which the proprietor had bought in good faith. However, the hot afternoon sun hitting the showcase brought the thin oily film to the surface and one "feel" was all the demonstration needed after the fact had been called to his attention. He withdrew the beads from stock.

Another test of suspected beads can be made by passing them through the flame of an alcohol lamp. The heat drives out the grease, or, if genuine, does not carbonize the stones.

Occasionally when a brown matrix is desired by the turquoise dyer he resorts to the use of a small brush and a bottle of iodine. The latter liquid soaks into the soft matrix and water will not wash it out. Repeated brushing with the medicament deepens the color and imparts a rich brown to the stone which is difficult to detect. The so-called "Persian turquoise nuggets" which are seen in many shops devoted to Oriental curios are said to be imported from Tibet. The poor grades of these stones are also dyed and the spidery black lines on the irregular lumpy beads are faked with carbon. Very little turquoise is actually imported from Persia.

Within the last few years glass imitation turquoise beads and earrings have invaded the Southwest from Czechoslovakia. At a short distance these tear drop earrings appear very convincing and the less wealthy Indians have adopted the importations in lieu of the more expensive stones. These imitations, in conjunction with base metal replicas of small Navajo *conchas*, rings, and bracelets, are sold in the five and ten cent stores in New Mexico, particularly in Gallup during the Intertribal Ceremonial. I purchased several of the latter objects in Gallup a year or so ago out of curiosity. The cards to which these "Indian jewelry" specimens were attached bore no maker's name or trademark, hence I am led to believe they were made in America. I believe it is compulsory for all foreign made goods to be stamped with the name of the country in which they originate. This is but another instance of wholesale chiseling on the part of gimcrack jewelry manufacturers who seek to destroy the Navajo native industry by such petty methods.

Reputable dealers and Indian traders frown upon the sham Navajo jewelry. They know it hurts the trade. Many of the traders are attempting to revive old forms. One sees an ever increasing number of simple fluted bracelets, the single bracelet, triangular in cross section, marked by a few stamped designs; the twisted wire bracelet and the flat, modestly stamped bracelet. Now if they would but reintroduce the engraved patterns which were cut on the flat surfaces with a sharp pointed steel tool, they would be achieving the simplicity of effect that marked the first products of the native silversmiths, East and West. The overabundant use of turquoise, which began between 1880 and 1900, has become more marked in recent years. As a result the rings and bracelets, blatantly garish with their large and small stones, reflect the innate bad taste of the white buyer. Left to themselves the true Navajo craftsmen would produce objects of beauty.

As the art stands today, it is rapidly approaching the end of its native cycle, if we may term this adopted craft a native one. It has already gone through the various stages through which Indian adaptations of similar bits of alien culture have passed, and unless some radical change occurs it will soon cease to be Indian in feeling and will have reverted entirely to the culture which gave it birth.

5: Summary

THE DATA PRESENTED in the foregoing pages may be briefly summarized thus:

The ancestry of Navajo silver ornament forms has its roots in the silver trade jewelry distributed to the tribes east of the Mississippi River after 1750, and in the Mexican-Spanish costume ornaments and bridle trappings of the late eighteenth and early nineteenth centuries.

Ornaments of brass, German silver, and copper were obtained by the Navajo from the Plains tribes and the mountain Ute prior to the actual manufacture of such items in good silver by the Navajo themselves. Among the ornaments thus obtained may be listed the fluted wide bracelets, the large, plain, and simply ornamented belt *conchas*, the simple round, wire bracelets, the bracelets triangular in cross section, the finger rings, and certain forms of earrings.

Ornaments derived from Spanish-Mexican sources were the pomegranate beads, miscalled the "squash blossom," "sun flower," etc., the round, flat, fluted, and ball-shaped buttons, the silver mounted bridles and the *naja*. The *naja* seems to have come to the Navajo from Mexico via the Southern Great Plains Indians and not directly from the Spanish in New Mexico.

Later American contributions were the small canteens, the powder chargers, and other miscellaneous forms since grown into a limitless array of tie clasps, book markers, teaspoons, cigarette trays, boxes and holders, brooches, etc.

Silver working by the Navajo themselves was learned from Mexican silversmiths, the first dated reference of such a smith in the Navajo country being November, 1853.

The first recognized native smith is Atsidi Sani (the Old Smith), known to the Mexicans as Herrero Delgadito (Little Lean Iron Worker), who may have had some rudimentary iron working instruction from a Mexican captive shortly prior to 1853 but who learned his silversmithing craft from the Mexican silversmith taken into the Fort Defiance region by Captain Henry L. Dodge in the year 1853.

By 1864 there were two or three Navajos making a limited amount of silver buttons and perhaps a few bracelets.

First examples of Navajo silversmithing were either plain or engraved. The first stamped designs, 1864–67, were copied from Mexican leather patterns made with crude native-made punches.

Evidence now on hand points to a meagre use of turquoise and native garnets as settings for silver rings and bracelets, 1880–1885.

The first American silver used by the Navajo was obtained from silver dollars furnished by the soldiers at Fort Defiance and new Fort Wingate. Mexican silver *pesos* were furnished for the first time by Chah-leh Sani (Old Charley), Charles Crary, who opened and operated the first trading post in the Navajo country near Ganado Lake in 1871–1872.

NOTES

[1] This list is compiled from the various references found scattered through innumerable historical accounts, journals of travel, official documents, etc. Moreover, concrete evidence of the type specimens distributed among these tribes is to be found in the thousands of brooches, arm bands, gorgets, head bands, etc. in the collections of the Museum of the American Indian, Heye Foundation; Ohio State Historical Society; Oshkosh Public Museum, Wis.; Neville Public Museum, Green Bay, Wis.; Fort Wayne Historical Society, Allen Co., Indiana; Museum of Anthropology, University of Michigan, Ann Arbor, Mich.; Connecticut Historical Society, Hartford, Conn.; U.S. National Museum, Washington, D.C.; Alabama Anthropological Society, Montgomery, Ala.; National Museum of Canada, Ottawa, Canada; New York State Museum, Albany, N.Y.; The University of Chicago (George Langford Collections); State Historical Museum, Wisconsin; Rochester Municipal Museum, Rochester, N.Y.; and the private collections of R. M. Harrington, San Fernando, Calif.; Dr. R. P. Burke, Montgomery, Ala.; Peter Brannon, Montgomery; Amos W. Butler, Indianapolis, Ind., and Ely S. Lilley of Indiana.

[2] Gillingham, Harrold E., Indian and Military Medals from Colonial Times to Date, pp. 100–101, Phila., 1927.

[3] Sir William Johnson Papers, Vol. II, p. 632, entry of Aug. 4, 1756, "To John of the Senecas 2 dollars to release a Silver Arm Band pawned for rum. . . . 16 (shillings)"

[4] Mss. Account Book, Baynton, Wharton & Morgan, Harrisburg, Pa. Papers in this book uncataloged, no pagination.

[5] Michigan Pioneer Historical Collections, Vol. 10, pp. 581, 632–633.

[6] Niles Weekly Register, Supplementary Vol. 16, 1819, statistical table (p. 97) compiled by Col. R. J. Meigs concerning the population, arts, crafts, etc. of the Cherokee Nation in 1809. In the same volume p. 104 is a note concerning the Creek Indians. . . . "The Creeks have few mechanical ideas. They manufacture household utensils and silver ornaments for the nose and ears but they are ill made, clumsy and exhibit no indication of ingenuity." By which token one might infer that the craft had not long been established among these people.

[7] McKenney, Thomas L., and Hall, James, History of the Indian Tribes of North America, three folio volumes, Vol. 1, p. 65.

[8] Hodge, F. W., Handbook of the American Indians, two volumes, Vol. 1.

[9] Westervelt, Frances A., The Final Century of the Wampum Industry in Bergen County, Papers and Proceedings, Bergen Co. Hist. Soc. No. 12, 1916–1917.

[10] Denig, Edwin T., 46th Ann. Rep't. B.A.E., Tribes of the Upper Missouri, p. 591.

[11] In partial substantiation of this we find Mooney 1898, pp. (318–319) reporting the account of the Kiowa sun dance for the summer of 1866, which ceremony was known that year as the *Han-kopdal Kado,* "Flat metal, i.e. Germany silver sun dance." It was held on Medicine-lodge Creek, near its mouth, in Oklahoma. "It was so called because a trader brought them at this time a large quantity of German silver, from which they made head-dresses, belts for women, bracelets, and other ornaments. German silver is known to the Kiowa as 'flat metal,' because it is furnished to them in sheets, which they cut and hammer into desired shapes. On both calendars the event is recorded in the same way, by the figure of a head pendant with silver discs placed near the medicine lodge. Such pendants were attached to the head of the scalp lock, and consisted of a strip of buffalo hide reaching nearly to the ground and covered along the whole length with a row of silver, copper or German silver disks, gradually decreasing in size toward the bottom, which was usually finished off with a tuft of bright-colored horsehair. They were called *gom-adal-ha-ngya,* 'back-hair-metal' and were highly prized by the warriors. This was not the first time the Kiowa had obtained German silver. In the old days these ornaments were made for them, of genuine silver, by Mexican silversmiths near the present Silver City, New Mexico."

In connection with Mooney's last statement there may be a possibility that some of the southern trade silver pieces were made by Mexican smiths, but those were copies of the original type specimens furnished in baser metals by American traders, hence the patterns would be those used by the Eastern tribesmen. It will be noted that Mooney does not give any dates for the manufacture of these Mexican ornaments.

A good photograph showing a Wichita girl in a costume which will date in the late 1860s or 1870s depicting a belt strap studded with round *conchas* and a profusion of bracelets on the arms is published by Mooney in an article, Quivira and the Wichitas, *Harper's Magazine,* June 1899, p. 129.

Other illustrations of silver hairplates will be seen in David I. Bushnell, Jr. Various Uses of Buffalo Hair, *Am. Anthropologist,* n.s. 11, July–Sept. 1909.

[12] Mooney, James, Calendar History of the Kiowa, 17th Ann. Rep't. B.A.E. Washington, D.C. 1898, pp. 255–257.

In January, 1833, the Kiowa fell upon a party of American traders returning from Santa Fe to Missouri and robbed the outfit of about $10,000 in silver specie.

"They found a few coins upon the ground, but this being the first money they had ever seen they did not know its proper use, and so beat the coins into disks to be fastened to straps worn attached to the scalp lock, and hanging down behind (hence the name for money *a'dalhan'gya,* literally 'hair metal'). After leaving the place they met some Comanche, who already knew the use of money, and on hearing the story told them of the value of the silver pieces, upon which the Kiowa returned and searched until they succeeded in finding a large quantity. From this it appears that whatever trade the Kiowa had previously carried on with the Spanish settlements had been by barter in kind as was usual along the Indian frontier in the early days. This was some time before the beginning of regular intercourse with Americans."

Thomas C. Battey in his, "The Life and Adventures of a Quaker Among the Indians," Boston, 1889, also speaks of the use of German silver among the Kiowa and shows Kiowa girls wearing silver *conchas* (p. 284).

[13] Gregg, Josiah, Commerce of the Prairies, Early Western Travels, Vol. 19, pp. 340–342, Cleveland, Ohio, 1905.

[14] Simpson, James H., Report of an Expedition into the Navajo Country in 1849. In Senate Ex. Doc. 64, 31st Cong. 1st Sess. Washington, 1850. (See various portraits of Navajo and Pueblo Indian leaders.)

Nebel, Carlos, Viaje Pintoresco y Arqueolojico sobre la parte Mas interesante de la republica, Mejicana, etc. desde 1829 hasta 1834.

[15] *Missouri Intelligencer,* Nov. 4, 1825, p. 3, cols. 2–3.

[16] One of the first, if not the first article on the Navajo by an American appeared in the *Missouri Intelligencer,* April 3, 1823, p. 3, cols. 2–3–4. For that reason it appeared worthwhile to reprint it verbatim.

Nabijos

Between the Spanish settlements of New Mexico and the Pacific Ocean reside a nation of Indian called the Nabijos, whose ingenuity and improvements reflect honor upon the uncivilized state. Their skill in manufacturing, and their excellence in some of the useful and ornamental arts, show a decided superiority of genius over all the other tribes of the western continent: even over those, whose contiguity to civilization, had afforded them the benefit of its example and instruction. That they are selftaught there is no doubt; and although our information is deficient relative to their origin, customs, manners and municipal regulations, perhaps it may enable us to state some facts concerning them interesting to our readers, and which may lead to more satisfactory intelligence.

It is believed by the Spaniards that they are a remnant of the ancient Mexican nation, under the government of the emperor Montezuma, who fled from their happy vales, beautiful lakes, and splendid towns; preferring to scent the fragrance of liberty and taste the sweets of domestic repose, in a distant wilderness, rather than submit to the dominion and cruelties of Cortes. To noble minds, rendered indignant by unprovoked wrongs, such a course would have been perfectly natural. But circumstances induce us to believe that supposition is incorrect. The barbarous disposition and destroying policy of a heartless invader, in a few years, laid in ruins that powerful and well-regulated empire; and swept from the face of the earth its numerous inhabitants, who were simple, happy and polished in a state of nature.

The miserable remains amalgamated with their conquerors; and their national character, peculiarity of customs, and pride of independence sunk together in a common grave. It is a more reconcilable supposition, that the Nabijos were originally a different nation, and one whose arts and mode of living have never been adulterated by an intercourse with civilized society. Their power and bravery are proverbial among the Spaniards, who have experienced more molestation and injury from them than from all the other Indians in their vicinity. They once sent to Santa Fe, a large quantity of silver bullion to be moulded into dollars, which the Spaniards perfidiously converted to their own use. The Spaniards also prohibited the cultivation and manufacture of tobacco among them, with a view to necessitate them to purchase their own for which they demanded an extravagant price. These, together with other causes of dissatisfaction, have for many years occasioned mutual hostilities, in which they usually triumphed over the pusillanimity of the Spaniards, and made a large proportion of their sheep and mules the spoils of war. A young gentleman, now in this town, accompanied a strong military expedition against them, which defeated them;

and obliged them to sue for peace. They killed a chief who wore shoes, fine woolen stockings, small-clothes, connected at the sides by silver buttons instead of a seam; a hunting shirt and a scarlet cloth cap, the folds of which were also secured by silver buttons.

These people do not adopt the usual Indian manner of living in villages, but are a nation of comfortable and independent farmers. Their houses are built of stone, some one, and other two stories high. They have fine flocks of sheep, abundance of mules, and herds of cattle of a superior kind. They cultivate corn, tobacco, and cotton which they manufacture into cloth. They have gardens in which they raise several kinds of esculent vegetables; and have peach orchards, the fruit of which resembles our apricots. Several articles of their woolen manufacture equal the quality of ours. We have seen a coverlet, made by them, the texture of which was excellent, the figures ingenious, and the colors permanent and brilliant. Our townsman, Mr. Hood, has taken it to Philadelphia for the purpose of sending it to a friend in Europe. The Spaniards imitate the manufacture of this article, but their imitations are far inferior to the original.

They make baskets, and small dishes of osiers, so compactly worked as to hold water without the least leakage. The twigs, before being wrought, are variously colored, and so skillfully put together that the finished vessel presents different figures.

Their bridles are made of tanned leather, and often embellished with silver ornaments. They dress almost wholly in their own fabrics. The men dress in small clothes, sometimes of deer skin, tanned and handsomely colored. The women wear a loose black robe, ornamented around the bottom with a red border, which is sometimes figured; and when not engaged they use a large shawl of the same color and material. Their different modes of putting up the hair, show whether they are single, lately married or matrons.

The weapons of this interesting nation are the lance, bow and arrow; which they use with dexterity.

These advantages and improvements among the uncivilized, if they may be so called, will no doubt astonish many; but the characters of those, who have given us the information, are so far above suspicion, that we should feel little reluctance in vouching for the truth of every fact. But there need be little surprise, when we reflect upon the character and conditions of the natives of that country when Europeans first visited them. They were well versed in the arts of painting, sculpture and architecture. Their gardens were large and well filled with medical and flowering plants and esculent roots. The city of Mexico, was at that time, more splendid and populous than any other in the world. Its population was more than 400,000; its houses were built of rock, and many of them three stories high. Its streets were wide, straight, and regularly laid off. They were furnished with water by canals, and the houses were also furnished by aqueducts. One of the emperor's palaces could conveniently accommodate 500 persons. Its walls were built of jasper of various colors, and beautifully polished; and its rooms were ornamented by cotton hangings and feathered tapestry, richly painted. Their works of art were numerous, and executed with the most consumate skill; and their public edifices and other works for public accommodation were grand and stupendous monuments of human ingenuity. When these things are considered it cannot be thought very strange that the Nabijos, inhabitants of the same country, should have attained to the improvements and degree of civilization which we have described.

This article was written by Nathaniel Patten, then editor of the *Intelligencer.*

The Mr. Hood to whom he refers was a Robert Hood, a merchant of Franklin who had a store on the east side of the Public Square where he sold dry goods, hardware and groceries, and took beeswax, flax, and tow linen in exchange for goods. (Ad in the *Intelligencer,* Jan. 11, 1825, p. 1, col. 3.)

Another item, also headed "The Nabijos," dated Franklin, Mo. April 10, 1824 which probably appeared in the *Intelligencer* was republished in the *Missouri Republican,* April 26, 1824, p. 2, col. 2. It contains less information but is interesting as an early sketch by an American writer.

"Since our last we have conversed with Mr. James Purcel, for 19 years a citizen of New Mexico and formerly of Pennsylvania. General Pike in the appendix to his journal through the interior provinces, devotes two pages in relating the circumstances of an interview with this man to whom he attributes 'strong sense and dauntless bravery.'

"Mr. Purcel's long residence there has given him an opportunity of knowing many particulars concerning the Nabijos whom he described last week both by observation and report.

"The character of the gentleman who gave us that information is a sufficient guarantee for its correctness. We will however, mention that the person above alluded to, confirms every part of the statement; and says it is perfectly free from exaggeration and expresses his unqualified admiration of the character of those Indians.

"They are much fairer than any other Indians in that country, and their features are different, being more commanding and expressive. Their flocks of sheep are extremely numerous and their cattle are the finest he ever saw. They select the most eligible situation over the surface of a large tract of country where they have excellent farms, which produce grains and fruits sufficient for a comfortable subsistence. Their wool is of a fine quality and their manufactures of wool and cotton equal the ordinary manufactures of those articles in other countries.

"Mr. Purcel is an illiterate man, but expresses a conviction, from their proficiency in the arts, their excellence in farming and their ingenuity in manufacturing that they are descendants of some civilized nation. This, however, is impossible. He relates a circumstance which goes far to prove their manliness and regard for principle. It will be recollected that in August 1822, Capt. Cole and his nephew were killed by those Indians on the bank of the Rio del Norte opposite a small Spanish town.

"The Nabijos discovered them in the evening, and had no doubt of their being Spaniards. They watched them from an elevated place and finding that they did not cross over, they took advantage of the night to murder them. The rifles and other equipment soon made it known that they had killed Americans instead of Spaniards, and the mistake filled them with grief. They did not strip them as they do their enemies, and left them a part of the baggage. Afterwards in a conversation with an American gentleman, they described, through an interpreter, their feelings on the occasion and mentioned, in emphatic language, the sorrow and regret which the mistake had occasioned them. They said that the few Americans they had seen always treated them kindly; that they were a good and brave nation, against whom they had no enmity; that they were distressed at killing their friends, and that after discovering the mistake, they went away mortified and displeased.

"This shews a nobleness of mind, a respect for our national character and a strong attachment to the principles of justice. We understand that the Spaniards and all the Indians that have intercourse with them, entertain a high regard for the Americans, and think them the most powerful, brave and enterprising people on earth."

[17] Bullock, W. Six Months in Mexico, London, 1825.

[18] Mss. depositions of Spanish soldiers in Pinart Collection, Bancroft Library, University of California, Berkeley.

[19] *Santa Fe Weekly Gazette,* Nov. 29, 1856, p. 2, col. 3; and March 14, 1857.

[20] *Santa Fe Weekly Gazette,* Dec. 11, 1858, p. 2, col. 1.

[21] Letterman (Letherman) Jonathan, Sketch of the Navajo tribe of Indians, Territory of New Mexico, Tenth Annual Report of the Smithsonian Institution, Washington, 1856.

[22] *Santa Fe Weekly Gazette,* Nov. 13, 1858.

[23] Ives, Lt. Joseph C., Report Upon the Colorado River of the West, Washington, D.C. 1861 (See plate on Navajos).

[24] Condition of the Indian Tribes. Report of the Joint Special Com-

mittee, appointed under Joint Resolution of March 3, 1865, with An Appendix. Washington, Government Printing Office, 1867, pp. 354–355.

[25] Ethnologic Dictionary of the Navaho Language, Franciscan Fathers, St. Michaels, Ariz., 1910, p. 271.

[26] Hodge, F. W., How Old is Southwestern Indian Silver-work? El Palacio, vol. 25, no. 14–17, pp. 224–232.

[27] This alloy known as German silver apparently came into general use between 1830 and 1835. It is composed of about 50% copper, 25% zinc and 25% nickel, for objects desired to take a high polish. It was originally made at Hildburghausen, Germany. The Encyclopaedia Britannica, vol. XI, N.Y. 1910.

[28] Travels of William Bartram, Philadelphia, 1791. . . . reprint Macy-Masius, N.Y. 1928, p. 393.

Beach, W. W. The Indian Miscellany, Albany, 1877, p. 326.

Carver, John Captain, Three Years Travels in the Interior Part of North America, etc. 1766, Phila. 1796, p. 147.

[29] Mooney, op. cit. An excellent example of one of these Plains woman's silver mounted belts is in the Los Angeles Museum collections.

[30] Mooney, p. 165, 170, 171–172.

[31] Mss. Pinart Collections.

[32] Harrington, M. R. Iroquois Silverwork, Anthropological Papers of the American Museum of Natural History, Vol. 1, Pt. VI, Sept. 1908.

Parker, Arthur. The Influence of the Iroquois on the History and Archeology of the Wyoming Valley, Pennsylvania, Proceedings of the Wyoming Historical and Geological Society, Vol. XI, pp. 28–31, Wilkesbarre, Pa., 1911.

[33] (See full quotations from manuscript on Pueblo clothing and weaving by Mrs. Matilda Stevenson, now on file in the Bureau of American Ethnology. Quotations on Zuñi and Navajo silversmithing supplied from a copy of this manuscript on file in the Denver Art Museum, courtesy of Mr. Frederic Douglas.) Although Mrs. Stevenson makes a positive statement that this was the *first* setting of turquoise in silver, one cannot help but query how did she know it was the first time it had been done? Her testimony is interesting and indicative of an early use of turquoise and silver by the Navajo but not conclusive. See the statement of Sam Tilden in the Supplement, regarding the setting of turquoise in silver by "Big Whiskers."

[34] Halsey, F. W. Four Great Rivers — Journal of Richard Smith 1769, Scribners, N.Y. 1906, pp. 68–69.

Jones, Rev. David. A Journal of Two Visits Made to Some Nations of Indians on the West Side of the River Ohio in the Years 1772 and 1773. Reprinted for Joseph Sabin, N.Y. 1865, p. 84.

[35] Specimens of such bridles are in the collection of the Museum of the American Indian, Heye Foundation.

See also comments by Miss Bedinger, Navajo Indian Silver-work, Denver, Colo. 1936, p. 33.

[36] Bedinger, id. p. 28 and 33.

[37] Ridgeway, W. The Origin of the Turkish Crescent, The Journal of the Royal Anthropological Institute of Great Britain and Ireland, v. XXXVIII, pp. 241–258 (with plates).

Other items on the horse trappings of England that serve admirably to illustrate the numerous forms of ornaments that have descended from these amulets are:

Carter, H. Robeson. English Horse Amulets, The Connoisseur, July, 1916, pp. 14–153.

Burgess, F. W. Chats on Old Copper and Brass, N.Y. n.d. pp. 370–371.

[38] Bedinger, id. p. 33.

[39] Matthews, Washington. Navaho Silversmiths, Second Ann. Rept. B.A.E. pp. 169–170, Washington, 1883. The same chargers are illustrated in Fig. 18, Navajo Legends, N.Y. 1897, by the same author.

[40] Leslie, Frank. The American Soldier in the Civil War. Bryan Taylor & Co., N.Y. 1895, p. 190.

Glossary of Spanish-Mexican Words

Botas — Knee length wrap-around leggings.

Conchas (shells) — Large oval or circular flat metal ornaments.

Conquistadores — Spaniards who conquered New Mexico in the sixteenth and seventeenth centuries.

Manta — Shawl or blanket.

Mochilas — Saddle bags.

Naja — Crescent shaped pendant. Derived from Navajo word *Nazháhi.*

Plateros — Silversmiths.

Poncho — Blanket with hole for head.

Ricos — Rich men.

Tapaderos — Leather cover of a stirrup.

APPENDIX No. 1

WHITE SILVERSMITHS
1736–1826

SILVERSMITHS who were engaged in manufacturing ornaments for the Indian trade in the eighteenth and nineteenth centuries are listed alphabetically; the dates indicate the years they are known to have supplied silver truck to traders and government officials.

Name	*Place*	*Date*
Burnett, Charles A.	Alexandria, Va.	1793 – 1824
Benjamin, John	Stratford, Conn.	1752
Bequette, Jean Baptiste	Fort Wayne, Ind.	1820
Bosworth, Samuel	Buffalo, N.Y.	1828 – 1838
Corbin, John	Stratford, Conn.	1750 – 1796
Cruickshank, Robert	Montreal	1779
Dangen, Antoine		1820
Dumoutet, John Baptiste	Philadelphia	1790s– 1800
Feuter, Daniel Christian	New York	1754 – 1769
Gother, Francis		1770
Griffin, Robert		1744
Kinzie, John	Detroit-Chicago	1785 – 1820

Leacock, John	Philadelphia	1748 - 1796
Leacock, Godfrey		1767
Letourneaux, M.	New York	1797
Loring, Joseph	Boston	1788 - 1796
Milne, Edmund	Philadelphia	1757 - 1813
Mix	Albany	1790s- 1816
Oneille, Antoine	Vincennes, Ind.	1803 - 1826
Payne, C. S.	Detroit	1820
Price, Benjamin	Philadelphia	1767
Ransom, Asa	Geneva, N.Y.	1789 - 1800
Ruland, Israel	Detroit	1773 - 1805
Scott, Robert	Virginia	1781
Simons, Joseph		1765
Ten Eyck, Barent	Albany, N.Y.	1764
Van Rensselaer, Jeremiah	Albany	1736
Wishart, Hugh	New York, N.Y.	1784 - 1810
Young, Benjamin	New York	1769

The foregoing list comprises the majority of the smiths known to have made the silver ware for Indians. Identification of these smiths has been made either from their touch marks on existing specimens or bills rendered for services. Likewise some have been named by eighteenth century officials who dealt directly with them. There are other smiths suspected of having performed similar work and many unidentified silversmiths whose marks appear upon ornaments recovered from Indian graves, but who as yet have not been identified.

A modern Navajo smith who stamps his ware FP superimposed upon an arrow is Fred Peshlakai, who in February, 1937 was working in an Indian curio store on Hollywood Boulevard, Los Angeles. Peshlakai said he was the son of Ansosi Peshlakai. Fred began stamping his wares thus about 1934 or 1935. He was vague as to the exact date he began. Prior to that time he said he stamped his wares with a small hogan as a trademark. No doubt other bona fide Navajo smiths have their own special marks. It would be interesting to compile a list with the dates for the reference of future students.

APPENDIX No. 2

NAVAJO SILVERSMITHS IN THE 1880s

TWO VERY ILLUMINATING accounts of the Navajo and Zuñi silversmithing describing the nature of the ornaments made and worn at that period have come to light recently. One of these is contained in the manuscript on Pueblo clothes and weaving by Mrs. Matilda Stevenson, which is deposited in the Bureau of American Ethnology, a copy of which is in the Denver Art Museum from which manuscript I have been furnished the following extracts by Mr. Frederic Douglas, Curator of Indian Art. The other item is embodied in the journal of Lt. J. G. Bourke as edited by Lansing R. Bloom, "Bourke on the Southwest," which is being issued in parts in the *New Mexico Historical Review.* The journal began in the issue for January, 1933, and at the time of this writing (Nov. 1937) is still being continued.

In April, 1881, Bourke visited the Navajo Agency at Fort Defiance, and the following observations were recorded by him in his journal for that month:

Both men and women are passionately fond of silver ornaments and being good workers in that metal, it need surprise no one to be told that many of the grown men and women, more particularly the former, are fairly loaded down with it. It is used as ear-rings, great circular loops, each containing at least one trade dollar; as belts to gird about the waist, as sashes to run across the breast and shoulder, as rings, as bangles (not infrequently can be seen a squaw with ten and eleven on each arm) as buttons to moccasins, leggings and last, but by no means least, to encrust their saddles and bridles. They make it into fantastic necklaces which contest the supremacy of their affections with chalchiuitl and red coral, the latter brought into the country during the Mexican domination. . . .

One of the old bucks in the store wore suspended by a chain from his waist belt, a silver tobacco pouch of simple but tasteful workmanship.

The scene was essentially barbaric, the dresses of the riders gorgeous and fantastic and the trappings of the ponies jingling with silver. None of the throng wore a hat — men and women wearing the hair alike — that is brushed smoothly back behind the ears and gathered into a knot above the shoulders; a bandana handkerchief or fillet of some kind keeping it in position. The display of coral and turquoise beads was something to excite astonishment, while those who were not the fortunate possessors of such heirlooms contented themselves with strands of silver hemispheres and balls of copper. Only pure metal is employed by the Navajo; plated ware he rejects at once.

Their neck-laces, bracelets, bangles and ear-rings are, as said above, of coral, chalchiuitl, or silver, sea-shells and malachite are seen at times, but silver may be regarded as the typical Navajo ornament. The ear-ring is inserted at the lower extremity of the lobe only; is made in the form of a simple solid ring and is fastened by a sliding button at the bottom. . . .

When Bourke left the Agency Mr. Leonard very kindly presented him "with a pair of silver bangles and a pair of silver bridle rosettes, all made by the Navajoes. . . ."

Lieutenant Bourke continued his journey to Zuñi and made a number of interesting observations over there. He saw some silver worn by the Zuñi:

Around the neck was a collaret reaching to the waist made of silver balls and quarter dollars and terminating in a pendant. . . . The moccasin of the Zuñis resembles that of the Navajoes in being fastened by silver buttons on the outside of the instep like our low quarter shoes. . . .

The brother of the *Gobernador* was described as . . . "a very dandified chap in pantaloons of black velvet, decked with silver buttons, a red shirt and a dark blue plush cap also girt with buttons of the precious metal." It is interesting to compare this description of a Zuñi man in May, 1881, with that of the Navajo described in 1824. Over half a century had elapsed, yet there was very little change in the costumes of the Navajo and Puebloan men.

While in Zuñi Bourke "Bought a pair of Zuñi ear-rings of same style as those of the Navajoes — paid for them $1.50."

In connection with metal working at Zuñi it is pertinent to mention the lithograph of a blacksmith shop in the Pueblo of Zuñi which appeared in "Report of an Expedition down the Zuñi and Colorado Rivers," by Captain L. Sitgreaves, Washington, 1853.

Mrs. Stevenson in her comments on Zuñi and Navajo silversmithing is, at times, not altogether historically correct. However, the following passages extracted from her manuscript are quoted verbatim.

Silversmiths sprang up who imitated the Spanish workers and with their crude forges, bellows, crucibles and dies they fashioned beads, crescents, buttons, crosses, bangles, finger rings and other ornaments.

In 1879 the Pueblo men (Zuñi) were wearing loose cotton trousers frequently confined at the waist by a leather belt strung with silver medallions of native workmanship.

The ornaments consisted of silver hoop earrings. . . . The full dress consisted of buckskin knee pants lined on the outer side with silver buttons, leggings of the same ornamented with silver buttons and a native blue woven shirt.

In 1879, except on ceremonial occasions, Zuñi women wore "A necklace of silver beads with a crescent pendant symbolizing the world, a few bangles and a silver ring or two."

Commenting on Navajo costume she stated "Their silver jewelry was more elaborate, no doubt, because the Navaho were the greatest silversmiths in the Southwest, having learned the craft as they did blanket weaving, from the Pueblos."

Again reverting to a general discussion of Zuñi and Navajo smithing she remarks:

Silver ornaments were introduced after the Spaniards brought coin into the country. Beads, finger rings and bangles were the first articles made of silver and were especially in view in ceremonials though they were seen at other times. The silver necklaces are for women and children, but men frequently wear them. After a time the beads were interspersed with small Latin crosses, and a double cross tipped with the "sacred heart" formed a pendant to the chain. This style or ornament was a favorite in Mexico and there are still fine specimens to be seen there. The crescent as a world symbol was introduced later. The silver squash blossom was a more recent achievement in the silversmith's art. Plain convex buttons have been in use for many years, but the fluted buttons made of United States coins — quarters, half dollars and dollars — beaten and chiseled, were the handiwork of the Navaho in the late seventies. Leather bow wristlets are ornamented with silver, and leather belts for men are strung with heavy elaborate silver medallions. Bridles are often quite covered with silver.

The first setting of turquoise in silver occurred in 1880. It was done by a Navaho in a ring which he presented to the writer.

Then the crescents were set with turquoise. These Indians (Navajo) became much interested in the setting of stones and the Zuñi followed after them and both tribes have produced most interesting specimens, the Navaho however, excelling the Zuñi in originality of design.

The Mexican dollar, owing to its purity, is employed by the silversmith in preference to the silver dollar of the United States.

In 1879 the furnace, bellows, crucibles and everything pertaining to the workshops of the silversmiths were of home manufacture except the old Mexican blow pipes, and carpenter's files and hammers. Coin is cut into bits and melted in pottery crucibles and run into a mold, the form depending on what is to be made. For a bangle the silver is formed into a slender rod which is hammered into shape and decorated with a file after patterns were made by the silversmith. Each style of button has its particular mold. The Navaho were the first to doctor the silver with a white metal introduced by traders and the Zuñi were not slow to follow.

A heavy copper wire introduced by American traders was worked to some extent by the Navaho, but it never found favor with the Zuñi.

APPENDIX No. 3

FIELD NOTES
By Richard Van Valkenburgh

FOREWORD—The following notes on Navajo silversmithing were obtained from several reliable native informants by Richard Van Valkenburgh of the Navajo Service, U.S.D.I. It will be observed that in the main, these independent statements concerning the origin of Navajo smithing and the ornaments themselves, corroborate or at least partially substantiate observations made elsewhere in this book. In arranging these items I have kept the spelling of the native names as indicated by Mr. Van Valkenburgh in his original copy.

—Arthur Woodward

Navajo Smiths 1850–1900

IRONSMITHS

1. Knife Maker, Old Smith, Herrero Delgadito — known as the most important iron smith 1850–1865. Lived near Nazlini and Fluted Rock.
2. Fat Smith. Lived beyond Chinlee.
3. Crying Smith
4. Big Smith. Lived at Fluted Rock. Did some silversmithing.
5. Grey-Streak-of-Rock-People Smith

6. Tall House. Fort Defiance.
7. Little Smith

SILVERSMITHS

1. Ugly Smith. Did first silversmithing with Mexican money on ridge west of Fort Defiance, Arizona. Made first headstalls and belts. Lived near Klagetoh. Made solid silver buttons with strips made from cartridge shells. All work heavy, and crude. Old discarded shovels were used to melt metal and the only tools were scissors, hammers, and files.
2. Silversmith. Nazlini, Arizona.
3. Always Hungry Old Silversmith (Slim Old Silversmith). Crystal, New Mexico.
4. Very Slim Silversmith (Very Slim Maker of Silver). Crystal, New Mexico. Innovator of new forms and refinement of silversmithing, particularly active in the 1880–1890s. Learned the art from Ugly Smith. Made first buckles, star-like buttons, flat type bracelets, and made first turquoise set for ring, for Chee Dodge. Said by Frank Walker and Chee Dodge to be the greatest of all silversmiths. Died 1916.
5. Shorty Silversmith (Silver Maker). Said to have made first hollow globular silver beads.
6. Maker, Silversmith.
7. Long Mustache. Said to have been the first to use garnets and turquoise (in the late 1880s). Went to World's Fair in 1893. Made his own dies and stamps. Lived at Bear Springs, four miles west of St. Michaels, Arizona.
8. Paper Carrier, Jake the Silversmith. Fort Wingate, New Mexico.

Vocabulary of a Few Navajo Words Referring to Metalworking

Belt — *sis*

Bow Guard — *keto*

Bracelet — *laht-sun* (hand metal)

Conchas — *ilth-dah-not-ahie* (something that holds)

Copper — beshleh cheé (red iron)

Earrings — *jah k'loth* (ear rope)

Iron — *besh*

Necklace — *yo* (bead)

Ring — *yos tso* (big bead)

Silver — *beshlah-k'ia* (white iron)

Tin — *beshk' ah-geé* (thin iron)

Statement of Sam Tilden, Born 1869

"We knew of worked silver, and a few of the *ricos* (rich men) had *concha* belts, some made of copper and some looked like silver with lots of copper in them. The *conchas* were usually plain, but some had one simple band of decoration around the edge. They traded these from the Utes, who, some say, got them from the Mexicans. I speak of before we were taken to Hwelte (Bosque Redondo). Of course, we knew of working with iron long before that. Herrero, first called Besh-ilth-ee-ni (Knife Maker), then Atsidi Sani (Old Smith), made things in iron. He lived near Nazlini and Fluted Rock and made bits, small chains, and plain *conchas.* Other iron smiths before the Navajo went to Hwelte were: Atsidi-Chai (Crying Smith); Atsidi Ilth-Kaa (Fat Smith); Atsidi Tso (Big Smith); Atsiidi Nah-Hoe-Bah-Ni (Gray-Streak-of-Rock-People Smith; Kin-ah-ah-ni (Tall House), also called Hastin Beh K'oh; and Atsidi Yazzi (Little Smith). It is said that Old Smith learned to work iron from a Mexican smith. I, Sam Tilden learned to work silver from Bee-daq-ee-nez (Long Mustache) 40 years ago, and he learned from 'Old Smith.'

"Herrero was the sixth man to sign the Treaty of 1868 at Hwelte. Of course these came after Herrero, who was really an ironsmith. 'Old Silversmith' and 'Slim Silversmith' were the best silversmiths of the early days. The early silver they kept for themselves. They would bring Mexican *pesos* to the silversmiths and paid one cow or horse for a big belt, two, five or six goats or sheep for bracelets and one goat or sheep for rings and ear circles. If they got any money from the army sutlers, they would never pay it back, they would just melt it up into silver.

"The first silver money that the Navajo got, came from the zxith-g'ahl*ee* — the White Mountain Apache. The first Mexican money came to us from Nah-k'ai-Sani (Old Mexican), Don Lorenzo Hubbell (1853–1930) . . . when I was about eight years old. (This was in 1877.) Before that Cha-l*ee* (Chas. Crary) who traded near Ganado Lake had some odd money which he said was an American dollar, but it was only about the size of a fifty cent piece today.

"Red and yellow garnets were set in silver before turquoise was used. The Navajo used to go up near Ganado and on Garnet Ridge near Dene-hotso and find them there. Garnet Ridge is a part of Comb Ridge. My teacher, Big Whiskers, had a woman at Santo Domingo Pueblo and used to hang around there all the time. He learned to set turquoise in silver from the Domingos. But at that time (about 1885) turquoise was hard to get, and not so very much was traded from the Domingos. Big Whiskers was the first Navajo known to me to set turquoise into silver. At first the stones were cut crudely, and then put into the object with the top flush with the cup (mounting of the bezel). Pieces were square and lozenge shape and sometimes just natural. Stones rising above the setting came in about 1900 when I had been smithing ten years."

Statement of Red Woman, Born 1833, Died 1937

I saw but one or two belts when I was a girl . . . and those belonged to the *ricos,* Beh-ni-nath-thlanee (His Eyes See Comanches), and Hahsteen H*ah*-tah *l'eé* (Mr. Medicine Man). They got them in trade with the Utes and would only wear them on special occasions. We had no silver at Hwelte — only a little copper. We had seen this same stuff in rolls, the year before the exile (1862) when it was issued by Red Shirt at Fort Defiance. Later at Fort Sumner — they started to flatten it out by pounding, and after looking at the Mexican decorations, took small pieces of pipe and cut them across the middle punching the copper thus  : but we did not have the tools to make the designs like the Mexicans. Then they started to mix up the punch marks and they got these patterns  and  . Of course we mixed dashes and dots with these. The more beautiful work with pretty punch marks came in when I was a grandmother (about 1870–1875). We made some cast iron. They poured the hot iron into carved pieces of *chet-chil,* Mountain oak, and then rubbed the objects smooth on sandstone. *Bix* (a kaolinic clay) was also used later for making moulds. It was also mixed with juniper berries and eaten in olden times.

The bellows were made from goat hide and the wooden part from Mountain oak and sometimes pinyon. Oak charcoal was favored to burn, and smiths used to pay men to burn it into charcoal for them. Coal was *never* used — it was taboo for fire. When they first began making silver in any quantity I was in my menopause (Van Valkenburg estimates this was around 1880 but it may have been between 1878 and 1883). All the smiths would get together at one place and would work a forge there. There was one that still stands at the mouth of Canon de Chelly. They used to hire boys to pump the bellows. Before Hwelte they had very little iron, and would melt anything they could get — horse shoes stolen from the Mexicans, or anything at all.

Note — This statement is particularly interesting in that it relates to some of the design elements so favored by the Navajo. Although Red Woman, "born in the year of Falling Stars," (1833) mentions the fact that the Navajo after looking at Mexican decorations, made their simple punches to imitate those designs, she does not specify the nature of the material upon which the Mexican motifs appeared. However, by a process of elimination, it would seem that the patterns thus copied were found on Mexican leather work, principally upon the saddle trappings. Likewise the fact that she mentions the use of copper, indicates the scarcity of silver during those early years of the trade. — A. W.

Statement of Very Slim Man, Born in 1853

Before we went to Hwelte, bands of our young men would cross the Rio Grande (Nak'ai Toh — Mexican Running Water) and go into the country of the *Nath-thlani* (Many Enemies), about three days eastward from Santa Fe. (This was in the vicinity of the upper reaches of the Canadian River.) There they stole horses belonging to the Comanche. On one of these trips, we were discovered by two of the enemy, and in the fight we killed them. Being *ah-nai* (aliens or enemies) we had no fear of their bodies, for we could be purified by *En-tah* when we returned home. Also, we had been sung over before leaving the Navajo country by Nah-tah-lith, the "Going-to-be-Headman." One Nath-lani had silver on him, two rings, one on each braid of his hair, and while these looked like silver, they were of lighter weight, and decorated with a swastika. We also took two *conchas* of the same stuff from the bridle. These were plain, with square holes to tie them to the leather. Across the center of these square holes was a thin bar.

We took a small copper spoon, and I kept it for many years, only using it for special occasions and not allowing anyone else to use it.

Note — In this account Very Slim Man relates occurrences in his father's day, as told to Very Slim Man, by his father. This story confirms the fact that German silver objects were obtained by looting from the southern Plains Indians as related elsewhere in this book. — A. W.

Statement of Henry Chee Dodge Hahsteen Deet-Sai, Interpreter

Capt. Dodge came to the Navajo country to live, two years after Fort Defiance was established (September, 1851). Of course he had been there before with Colonel Washington in 1849. He built himself a stone house in Cottonwood Pass (now erroneously called Washington Pass). The Navajo call this place Bes-l'chee Beh geezh (Red Metal or Copper Pass). With him there was a Mexican smith who taught the Navajo around there to work iron and copper into nice shapes. Herrero came up to look on and learned some things. Capt. Dodge was killed down by Atarque by the Chiricahua Apache, the "Chis-eh," two years after he came to the Navajo country. He went on a hunting trip with some Navajo headmen, and after making camp one evening, went over a little hill to hunt. He didn't come back, and the Navajo went out to hunt for him, and found him dead and mutilated. They just left him there.

Note — In this account given by one of the most famous of the present Navajo headmen, the presence of Captain Henry L. Dodge in the Navajo country is verified and his death at the hands of the Apache is related substantially as it occurred. While it was true that the Navajo with whom Dodge was hunting at the time did leave the remains in the snow where they were found by the Indians, the military authorities later removed the fragmentary remains to the post cemetery at Fort Defiance where Editor Sam Yost later saw his grave in September 1858. The inscription upon the head board read:

"To the Memory of H. L. Dodge, Aged 45 years. Agent of the Navajos. Killed by Apache Indians on the 15th day of Nov. 1856. A portion of his remains rest beneath this spot."

It seems pertinent at this point to note that Henry (Chee) Dodge is not named after Captain Dodge. In fact I am given to understand that originally Chee Dodge's name was Dodd, not Dodge.

Whereas in the main, Chee Dodge's account is substantially correct, the reader is referred to Captain Dodge's own account of his entry into the Navajo country. It is remarkable that in spite of the lapse of eighty-one years, the memory of Captain H. L. Dodge has been kept remarkably fresh and the errors that have crept into the tradition of his coming, the Mexican smith that was with him, and the details of his death, are, after all, negligible. It will be noted that the Mexican silversmith is spoken of as the blacksmith, and the American blacksmith, George Carter has apparently been forgotten. Herrero is mentioned as having come to the agency to "look on" at the forge of the Mexican smith and "learned some things." Possibly the Mexican slave mentioned by Sam Tilden may have taught Herrero only the rudiments of the blacksmith's art. Lack of tools and material may have prevented any consistent practice on Herrero's part and the arrival of the American agent and his two smiths was just the impetus needed to bring the craft to fruition.

From Herrero's own account, previously quoted, we know that in 1865 he was able to do a limited amount of iron smithing, hence it seems fairly reasonable to assume that during the years 1853 to 1865 he had not launched forth any too industriously into the intricacies of either the blacksmith's or silversmith's art. It was only after the return from Bosque Redondo and subsequent settlement of affairs that Herrero and the other smiths, who must have been but a scant handful at that time, really became active in this field.

The scarcity of the precious metal between the 1860s and 1880s, that interim when the American traders had not yet firmly established themselves, may have caused a recession in the craft.

This is partially borne out by the statement of Mr. C. N. Cotton in a letter to Mr. Van Valkenburgh. The former stated that in 1884, he and Mr. J. L.

Hubbell imported Mexican silversmiths into Ganado to teach the Navajo the art. Moreover, until the traders developed a market among the whites the craft languished, the bulk of the ornaments being made for home consumption among the Navajo themselves. The ornaments taken into the trading posts prior to 1900, which more or less marks the boom of the tourist trade, were often treated as bullion by the traders. Cotton shipped a mass of this silver ware to the Denver mint in 1898 and received for it the sum of $800.

Additional comments upon the increased use of silver ornaments among the Navajo during the late 1880s and early 1890s were made by Mr. C. E. Vandever, Agent to the Navajo in a report dated June 30, 1890, now on file in the Fort Defiance agency records.

Excerpts from this report are quoted by Van Valkenburgh:

"The only money they will accept in traffic is silver coin, which is natural enough, as with paper currency they could readily be deceived, while they are excellent judges of silver. However, in the last year they have been willing to accept paper money. They melt from a third to a half of the coin they receive to make into silver ornaments, but for gold they have no appreciation. While they were poor they were content with brass, but with the coming of the railway and better markets for their products, they grew rich, and these yellow metals were discarded, and gold they reckon in the same category. Besides their first really valuable ornaments were of silver, and the Navajo ideal of splendor is the Mexican vaquero in gala attire, horse and rider heavily bedecked with silver."

It is curious but Vandever's remarks concerning the Navajo acceptance of brass and then the disdainful discarding of the metal, and the classification of gold in the same category with the baser metal, parallels the experience of the tribesmen of the far Eastern Woodland. During the seventeenth century the Iroquois, Delaware and other Indians who traded with the white men accepted brass and copper readily enough as ornaments, but as soon as silver was introduced, ca. 1730–1740, the yellow trinkets went more or less into the discard, and gold was relegated to the same class as the brass. On the Plains where brass was introduced later, and where the best quality of silver did not penetrate to any great extent, brass remained in favor, particularly the bracelets, finger rings (plain and set with colored glass),; thimbles for jinglers; tacks for ornamentation of gun butts, war clubs, saddles, mirror frames, etc.; buttons and wire. — A. W.

Statement of Chis-Chillie, Born near Black Mt. in 1855

The first silver belt was made by Atsidi Chon (Ugly Smith) at Fort Defiance in 1868 or 1869. This man also made the first silver headstall. He learned smithing from the Mexicans around Santa Fe and on the Pecos River. Silversmithing really began about the time the sheep were issued by "Big Belly" (Captain F. T. Bennett) and about the time "Little Gopher" (Major Theodore Dodd) died. The silver pesos were first introduced by a white man, "Chah-leh Sani" (Old Charley).

Note — Chah-leh Sani was Charles Crary who opened and operated the first trading post in the Navajo county in 1871–1872 at Ceh-tay-he-khaw, near Ganado Lake. Before the Navajo obtained the Mexican silver they used American dollars furnished by the soldiers of Fort Defiance and new Fort Wingate. — Van Valkenburgh

Statement of Cosonelo — Fort Wingate

"Big Lipped Mexican" came from Cubero, N.M. in the 1870s and taught the Navajo silversmithing. He was associated with Navajo smiths, particularly Slim Old Silversmith of Crystal and a brother, the famed Slim Silversmith. He made ornaments for them, as well as showing them some of the fine points of the craft. — Frank Walker

APPENDIX No. 4

Statement of Peshlakai Atsidi

Interpreted by Clyde Peshlakai and Edmund Nequatewa to Mary-Russell F. Colton September 3, 1937

Peshlakai Atsidi, a well-known medicine man, is eighty-seven years old. He and his family live on the west side of the Little Colorado River between the Wupatki National Monument and the Coconino Point where there is very slight contact with the outside world. His mind is exceedingly clear and his memory remarkable in almost every case.

Peshlakai stated that the first smiths that he ever saw were working iron, making Spanish bridles, etc., and that this was at Fort Sumner in New Mexico (in 1864), and that at the time he was twelve years old. He understood that these smiths were Mexicans.

He further stated that at first there was no white metal (silver); that the first buttons and *conchas* used as belts were made of yellow metal (brass and copper), that these were made without solder and were attached to the leather of the belt by lacing the leather through slots in the *conchas.* These metal *conchas* were first seen by the Navajos on the Utes. The Utes were bad men, killing and fighting. The Navajos called them "The Buckskin Shirts."

The first of these that he saw was worn by a Ute who was killed in a fight by his people and when he toppled off his horse they found a *concha* belt around his waist and his buckskin shirt was decorated with buttons. These buttons and the *conchas,* he declares, were decorated around the edges with the same type of decoration which we see today in the old slot *conchas.* The Utes knew nothing of solder.

Peshlakai declared that no turquoise were used in these pieces nor in the first silver that he can remember. He recalls that the bracelets which the Navajos wore before they used metals were made of deer horn which was boiled and bent when pliable. These were drilled with a bone awl and set with turquoise in pinyon gum.

Peshlakai says that the first white metal that he ever saw made into belts and buttons was at the Hubbell Post at Ganado. These first pieces of white metal were also of the slot type without solder.

Peshlakai says that it was at Don Lorenzo Hubbell's store at Ganado that a man whose name was Benedito first taught and encouraged the Navajo to make silver jewelry and to use solder. He says that the Mexicans were very jealous of their knowledge of making solder and did not wish the Navajos to learn, but that Benedito helped them.

Atsidi Sani or Old Smith mentioned in the Ethnologic Dictionary as possibly the first Navajo silversmith was known to Peshlakai who says that he lived close to Keams Canyon but he said several times very firmly that this man worked only in iron, making Spanish bridles, etc. At the same time there was an older man also a smith, named Dogache' or Red Whiskers. This man was a contemporary and great friend of Peshlakai Atsidi. He stated that they worked together, sharing their knowledge and that it was Dogache' who first found out how to make solder. It was very difficult to make solder for you had to have a yellow metal and a white metal together and to make them as one it was necessary to have alum. When they discovered this and learned to make it, all was well. Dogache' made a bellows out of buffalo hide (buckskin) and this was, he considered, a great achievement.

Peshlakai says further, that if any one says that Atsidi Sani was the first Navajo smith to make white metal, he is a liar, for it was Dogache' and himself working together who made the first white metal and learned to solder, with the help of Benedito.

He stated that he believes that Atsidi Sani died some fifty years ago.

Peshlakai also told of making some iron ear rings which were cut out from flat pieces of iron like those illustrated in the Mindeleff collection at the U.S. National Museum. When shown a picture from the National Museum, of a Navajo silversmith whose name was given as Boi-ie-schluch-a-ichin, the old man looked at this picture a long time, he thought he could remember him, and that he had died a long time ago and he remembered his name as Peshlagai-ilim altsosigi (Slender Silversmith).

Note — This statement is interesting in that it corroborates from the native point of view other remarks made in the body of this book.

Peshlakai Atsidi being twelve years of age in 1864 probably did not know of the two smiths taken to Fort Defiance in 1853, hence his testimony that he understood the first smiths he saw engaged in making iron work at Fort Sumner in the summer of 1864, were Mexican smiths, is probably correct. On August 22, 1864 the Assistant Adjutant General Ben C. Cutler in Santa Fe directed the dispatch of "a set of blacksmith tools complete, and some iron, to be sent to Fort Sumner for the use of the Navajoes. Tell them to go to work at once and make adobes to build the shop. You select the site near the post, and have the shop made long enough to have a forge in each end." (Report of the Joint Special Committee on the Condition of the Indian Tribes, Washington, D.C., 1867, p. 191.) Only one blacksmith was reported working at Fort Sumner during the months of March, April and May, 1865. He received a salary of $65 a month but his nationality is not disclosed. During the same period the blacksmith shop received 500 pounds of assorted iron, 1,000 pounds of assorted steel, 200 bushels of charcoal as well as a miscellaneous assortment of borax, tools, etc. (Id., p. 353).

The observations of Peshlakai Atsidi relative to the first *concha* belts likewise confirm previous statements that these were first used by the Plains and Ute Indians. Moreover the simple marginal decorations of those *conchas* are yet to be seen on old Plains belts, an example of which may be seen in the Los Angeles Museum.

However, it would seem that some of Peshlakai's final statements concerning the first manufacture of "white metal" objects are open to question. He states that himself and Dogache' working together made the first silver objects. This is obviously impossible unless Peshlakai began silversmithing as a boy of ten or eleven. We know from contemporary evidence, already cited, that there were Navajo silversmiths making a limited quantity of silver jewelry in 1863–1864. It may well be that Atsidi Sani or Old Smith mentioned by Peshlakai Atsidi did make iron bridles of Spanish type but other informants have also credited this same smith with having worked silver. It would seem that Peshlakai Atsidi's chronology is a bit confused. He mentions the fact that it was a Mexican silversmith Benedito at Don Lorenzo Hubbell's store who first taught and encouraged the Navajo to make silver jewelry and to use solder. Don Lorenzo moved to Ganado about 1879–1880 (Amsden, Charles. Navaho Weaving. *The Fine Arts Press,* Santa Ana, 1934, p. 175). Hence this is fifteen years after known dates when the Navajo were making silver ornaments and twenty-six years after Captain

Dodge took a Mexican silversmith and American blacksmith into the Fort Defiance region.

Peshlakai stated that Dogache made his bellows of buffalo hide which the interpreter thought must be buckskin. Mr. Frederic Douglas mentioned that there is at Zuñi an old bellows made of buffalo hide, at the present time.

Hence one may infer that while the statements of Peshlakai Atsidi contain many well grounded fundamental facts concerning the introduction of certain prototypes of Navajo ornaments into the Navajo country, his observations concerning the first manufacture of such items are true insofar as he himself is concerned but erroneous when applied to the art as a whole. — A. W.

BIBLIOGRAPHY

ALISON, E. V.
1911 Brass Amulets. The Connoisseur. London. October, 1911.

AMERICAN STATE PAPERS
1832–1834 Class II, Vols. I and II. Indian Affairs. Washington, D.C.

BARTRAM, WILLIAM
1791 Travels of William Bartram. Philadelphia, Pa. Reprint Macy-Masius, New York City, N.Y., 1928.

BAUDOUIN, DR. MARCEL
1927 La Prehistoric du Coeur. Biologie Medicale, Vol. XVII, No. 5, Paris, France, May, 1927.

BEAUCHAMP, WILLIAM
1889 Rarer Indian Relics of New York. The American Antiquarium. Chicago, Ill. March, 1889, pp. 110–116.
1903 Metallic Ornaments of the New York Indians. Bulletin 73, New York State Museum, Albany, N.Y.

BEACH, W. W.
1877 The Indian Miscellany. Albany, N.Y., p. 326.

BEDINGER, MARGERY
1936 Navajo Indian Silver Work. Old West Series of Pamphlets No. 8, John Van Male, Denver, Colo. (This is the most complete paper yet

published on the technical processes of Navajo smithing. It is a valuable supplement to Washington Matthews' earlier work.)

BELDEN, BAUMAN L.
1927 Indian Peace Medals. The American Numismatic Society, New York City, N.Y.

BLAKE, WILLIAM P.
1899 Aboriginal Turquoise Mining in Arizona and New Mexico. The American Antiquarian, Chicago, Ill. Sept.–Oct. 1899, pp. 279–284.

BOURKE, J. G.
1933 Bourke on the Southwest. Edited by Lansing B. Bloom. New Mexico Historical Review, Vol. VIII, No. 1, Santa Fe, N.M., Jan. 1933. (Serial of Bourke's journal continued to date, Oct. 1937.) Navajo silver mentioned Chap. XV, Jan., 1936.

BROWN, CHARLES E.
1918 Indian Trade Implements and Ornaments. The Wisconsin Archaeologist, Vol. 17, No. 13, Sept., 1918. Milwaukee, Wis.

BRANNON, PETER A.
1934 Indian Traders in the Alabama Country, Alabama Highways, Sept.–Oct., 1934. Montgomery, Ala.
1934 Pocket Knives and Looking Glasses. Alabama Highways, Nov.–Dec., 1934. Montgomery, Ala.
1935 The Southern Indian Trade. The Paragon Press, Montgomery, Ala. (All of these items pertain to various trade objects, including silver.)

BURGE, MORIS
1934 The Silversmithing of the Navajos. Indians at Work, U.S. Bur. Ind. Aff., Washington, D.C., Dec. 15, 1934.

BURGESS, F. W.
1934 Chats on Old Copper and Brass. New York City, N.Y., n.d., pp. 370–371. (Deals with horse trappings in Europe.)

BURKE, DR. R. P.
1934 A Rare George Washington Medal. Hobbies, Chicago, Ill. Feb. 1934.

CARTER, F. ROBESON
1916 English Horse Amulets. The Connoisseur, London, England. July 1916. pp. 143–153.

CARVER, CAPT. JONATHAN
1796 Three Years Travel in the Interior Part of North America, etc., 1766. Philadelphia, Pa.

CHAPMAN, KENNETH M.

1936 Zuñi Silversmithing. Indians at Work, U.S. Bur. Ind. Aff., Washington, D.C., Sept. 15, 1936. pp. 16–19.

CHITTENDEN, HIRAM

1902 The American Fur Trade of the Far West. New York City, N.Y.

CONVERSE, HARRIET MAXWELL

1900 Iroquois Silver Brooches. 54th Ann. Rep't. N.Y. State Museum, Albany, N.Y.

COUES, ELLIOTT

1895 Major Z. M. Pike, An Account of Expeditions to the Sources of the Mississippi and through the Western Parts of Louisiana to the Sources of the Arkansaw, Kans, La Platte and Pierre Jaun Rivers, etc. F. P. Harper, New York City, N.Y.

CUMBERLAND, F. BARLOW

1904 The Oronhyatekha Historical Collection. I.O.F. Catalog and Notes, Toronto, Canada.

CURTIS, EDWARD

1907 The North American Indian. Vol. 1, Apache, Jicarillas, Navajo. Cambridge, Mass.

1930 The North American Indian. Vol. XIX. Wichita, Southern Cheyenne, Oto, Comanche. Cambridge, Mass.

CUSHING, FRANK

1920 Zuñi Breadstuff. Indian Notes and Monographs, Vol. VIII. Museum of the American Indian, Heye Found., New York City, N.Y., pp. 553–534.

DAVIS, W. W. H.

1857 El Gringo; or New Mexico and Her People. Harper and Bros., New York City, N.Y.

DENIG, EDWIN T.

1929 Tribes of the Upper Missouri. 46th Ann. Rep't, B.A.E., Washington, D.C., p. 591.

DODGE, COL. RICHARD

1882 Our Wild Indians. A. D. Worthington and Co., Hartford, Conn.

EISEN, DR. GUSTAV

1898 Long Lost Mines of Precious Gems are Found Again, etc., San Francisco Call, March 18–19 and 27, 1898. (Refers to turquoise mines in Mojave Desert, Calif.)

ENSKO, STEPHEN
1927 American Silversmiths and Their Marks. Privately printed, New York City, N.Y.

FENTON, WM. N. and HILL, CEPHAS
1935 Reviving Indian Arts Among the Senecas. Indians at Work, U.S. Bur. Ind. Aff., Washington, D.C., June 15, 1935.

FRANCISCAN FATHERS
1910 Ethnologic Dictionary of the Navajo Language. St. Michaels, Ariz.

FURBER, GEORGE C.
1850 The Twelve Months Volunteer. J. A. and U. P. James, Cincinnati.

GILLINGHAM, HARROLD E.
1927 Indian and Military Medals from Colonial Times to Date. Address delivered before the Historical Society of Pennsylvania. Philadelphia, Pa.
1934 Indian Silver Ornaments. The Pennsylvania Magazine of History and Biography, Vol. LVIII, April, 1934.

GORDON, ELEANOR LYTLE KINZIE
1910 John Kinzie, "The Father of Chicago." Chicago, Ill., 1910.

GREGG, JOSIAH
1905 Commerce of the Prairies. Early Western Travels, Vol. 19. Arthur H. Clark Co. Cleveland, Ohio.

GRISWOLD, BERT J.
1927 Fort Wayne, Gateway of the West. Indiana Hist. Coll., Indianapolis, Ind.

HALSEY, F. W.
1906 Four Great Rivers. Journal of Richard Smith, 1769. Scribners, New York City, N.Y.

HARRINGTON, M. R.
1908 Iroquois Silverwork. Anthropological Papers of the American Museum of Nat'l. Hist., Vol. I, Part VI, Sept. 1908. New York City, N.Y.
1908 Vestiges of American Culture among the Canadian Delawares. American Anthropologist, N.S., Vol. 10, No. 3.

HECKEWELDER, J. G. E.
1819 History, Manners and Customs of the Indian Nations who once Inhabited Pennsylvania. Transactions of the American Philosophical Soc., Vol. I, Philadelphia, Pa.

HODGE, F. W.
1910 Handbook of American Indians, 2 vols. Bull. 30, B.A.E., Washington, D.C.

1928 How Old is Southwestern Indian Silverwork? El Palacio, Vol. 25, Nos. 14–17, Oct. 6–27. Santa Fe., N.M.

HOUGHTON, FREDERICK
1922 The Archaeology of the Genesee Country. Researches and Transactions of the New York State Archaeological Ass'n, Lewis H. Morgan Chap., Vol. III, No. 2, Rochester, N.Y. Pls. XVI–XVII

ILLINOIS HISTORICAL COLLECTIONS
Illinois State Hist. Library. Springfield, Ill.

INDIANA HISTORICAL COLLECTIONS
Hist. Bur. Ind., Library and Hist. Dept., Indianapolis, Ind.

INDIAN ARTS AND CRAFTS BOARD
1937 Indian Silver Work Standards. Indians at Work, U.S. Bur. Ind. Aff., Washington, D.C., March 15, 1937. (Report of Indian Arts and Crafts Board)

JAMES, GEN. THOMAS
1916 Three Years Among the Indians and Mexicans. Missouri Hist. Soc., St. Louis, Missouri.

JOHNSON, SIR WILLIAM
1925 Papers. Vols. I–VIII. Univ. of the State of N.Y., Albany, N.Y.

JONES, DR. CHAS. C.
1881 Silver Crosses from an Indian Grave-Mound at Coosawattee Old Town, Murray County, Georgia. Smithsonian Ann. Rep't 1880. pp. 619–624.

JONES, WILFORD
1936 How I Make A Silver Navajo Ring. Indians at Work, U.S. Bur. Ind. Aff., April 15, 1936, p. 31.

KETCHUM, WILLIAM
1864 Buffalo and the Senecas. Buffalo, N.Y.

KINZIE, MRS. JULIETTE A.
1901 Waubun or Early Days in the Old Northwest. Rand, McNally Co., Chicago, Ill.

LEWIS, J. OTTO
1835 The Aboriginal Portfolio — A Collection of Portraits of the Most Celebrated Chiefs of the North American Indians, 72 colored plates. Philadelphia, Pa.

LOSKIEL, G. H.
1794 History of the Missions of the United Brethren Among the Indians in North America. London, England.

LUMMIS, CHARLES
1896 Our First American Jewelers. Land of Sunshine, July, 1896. Los Angeles, Calif.

MATTHEWS, WASHINGTON
1883 Navajo Silversmiths, 2nd Ann. Rep't, B.A.E., Washington, D.C.

McKENNEY, THOMAS L. and HALL, JAMES
1854 History of the Indian Tribes of North America, 3 folio vol. Philadelphia, Pa.

MICHIGAN PIONEER HISTORICAL COLLECTIONS
Michigan Pioneer and Hist. Soc., Lansing, Mich. (Various volumes containing many lists of trade goods including silver ornaments.)

MISSOURI INTELLIGENCER
1824–1825 Franklin, Missouri. Various issues.

MOONEY, JAMES
1898 Calendar History of the Kiowa. 17th Ann. Rep't, B.A.E., Washington, D.C.

MOOREHEAD, WARREN K.
1887 Silver Find. The American Antiquarian, May 1887. Chicago, Ill.

MORGAN, LEWIS H.
1851 League of the Ho-de-no-sau-nee or Iroquois, Rochester, N.Y., Reprint, New York City, N.Y., 1922.

Navajo Silversmithing. Indians at Work, U.S. Bur. Ind. Aff., Washington, D.C., Oct. 15, 1936. (Reprinted from Art Series, No. 7, New Mexico Ass'n on Ind. Aff., Santa Fe, N.M.)

NEUMANN, DAVID L.
1932 Navajo Silverwork. El Palacio, Vol. 32, Santa Fe, N.M., Feb. 24, 1932, pp. 102–108.
1933 Navajo Silver Dies. El Palacio, Vol. 35, Santa Fe, N. M., Aug. 16–23, 1933. p. 71.

NILES WEEKLY REGISTER
1819 Supplementary Vol. 16.

OAKES-JONES, CAPT. H.
1922–1923 The Evolution of the Gorget. Journal of the Society of Army Historical Research, Vol. I, No. 3, Mar., 1922 to Vol. II, No. 7, 1923. Sir W. C. Leng and Co., Ltd., Sheffield, England.

O'CALLAGHAN, E. B.
1853–1887 Documents Relative to the Colonial History of the State of New York. Argus Co., Albany, N.Y.

PARKER, ARTHUR
1910 Origin of Iroquois Silversmithing. Amer. Anthropologist, George Banta Pub. Co., Menasha, Wis. July–Sept. 1910, n.s., Vol. 12, No. 3.
1911 Additional Notes on Iroquois Silversmithing. Amer. Anthropologist, George Banta Pub. Co., Menasha, Wis. n.s., Vol. 13, 1911.
1911 The influence of the Iroquois on the History and Archaeology of the Wyoming Valley, Pennsylvania. Proceedings of the Wyoming Historical and Geological Society, Vol. XI. Wilkes-Barre, Pa.

PELL, STEPHEN H. P.
1937 The Gorget as a Defense, as a Symbol and as an Ornament. The Bulletin of the Fort Ticonderoga Museum, Vol. IV, No. 5. Fort Ticonderoga, N.Y., Sept. 1937.

QUIMBY, GEORGE I., JR.
1936 Notes on Indian Trade Silver Ornaments in Michigan. Papers of the Michigan Academy of Science, Arts and Letters, Vol. XXII, 1936. Univ. of Mich., Ann Arbor, Mich.

RIO ABAJO WEEKLY PRESS
1863–1864 Albuquerque, N.M. Various issues.

ROGERS, MALCOLM
1929 Report of an Archaeological Reconnaissance in the Mohave Sink Region. The San Diego Museum, Archaeology, Vol. 1, No. 1. February, 1929.

SANTA FE WEEKLY GAZETTE
1853–1858 Santa Fe, N.M. Various issues.

SCHOOLCRAFT, HENRY R.
1854 Information Respecting the History, Condition and Prospects of the Indian Tribes of the U.S. Pt. IV. Philadelphia, Pa., 1854.

SHAW, HELEN LOUISE
1931 British Administration of the Southern Indians. Appendix A. Bryn Mawr College, Bryn Mawr, Pa.

SIMPSON, JAMES H.
1850 Report of an Expedition into the Navajo Country in 1849. Senate Exec. Doc., 64, 31st Cong., 1st Sess. Washington, D.C., 1850.

SLOAN, JOHN and LA FARGE, OLIVER
1931 Introduction to Amer. Ind. Art, Pt. 1, Exposition of Indian Tribal Arts, Inc., New York City, N.Y.

SPECK, FRANK
1909 Ethnology of the Yuchi Indians. Anthropological Pub. of the Univ. Mus., Univ. of Pa., Vol. 1, No. 1. Philadelphia, Pa.

1909 The Mohegan and Niantic Indians. Anthropological Papers of the American Museum of Natural History, Vol. III, Amer. Mus. Nat. Hist., New York City, N.Y.

SPENCER, O. M.

1917 The Indian Captivity of O. M. Spencer. Edited by Milo Quaife, The Lakeside Press, Chicago, Ill.

STEVENSON, MRS. MATILDA COX

Manuscript on Pueblo Clothing and Weaving, Bur. Amer. Ethnology, Washington, D.C.

1904 The Zuñi Indians, 23rd Ann. Rept. B.A.E., Washington, D.C. pp. 369–370, 377.

WEST, LOUIS C.

1935 Standards for Silver Jewelry. Indians at Work, U.S. Bur. Ind. Aff., Washington, D.C., Nov. 1, 1935.

WOODWARD, ARTHUR

1926 Indian Use of the Silver Gorget. Indian Notes, Vol. 3, No. 4, Museum of the Amer. Ind., Heye Foundation, New York City, N.Y., October, 1926.

1928 Mss. The Use of Silver Ornaments Among the Indians East of the Mississippi. Archives, Museum of the Amer. Ind., Heye Foundation. Written 1928.

1932 The Value of Indian Trade Goods in the Study of Archaeology. The Pennsylvania Archaeologist, Vol. 3, No. 1, Bull. Soc. for Pennsylvania Archae., Harrisburg, Pa., May, 1932.

1933 The Montreal Medal. The Bulletin of the Fort Ticonderoga Museum, Vol. 3, No. 1. Fort Ticonderoga, N.Y. January, 1933.

Selected Additions to the Bibliography

Publications from 1938 and after

ADAIR, JOHN

1944 Navajo and Pueblo Silversmiths. Norman: Univ. of Oklahoma Press.

BAHTI, TOM

1964 An Introduction to Southwestern Indian Arts and Crafts. Flagstaff: KC Publications.

BENNETT, EDNA MAE

1966 Turquoise and the Indian. Denver: Sage Books, Alan Swallow.

CLARK, LA VERNE H. C.

1963 Early Horse Trappings of the Navajo and Apache Indians. Arizona and the West, v. 5, no. 3, Autumn 1963. p. 233–248.

DOCKSTADER, FREDERICK J.
1953 The Centenary of Navajo Silversmithing. Cranbrook Institute of Science News Letter, Vol. 23, no. 2, October 1953, pp. 14–18. Bloomfield Hills, Michigan.

DOUGLAS, FREDERIC H.
1938 Navajo Silversmithing. Denver Art Museum, Indian Leaflet series no. 15, 1930 (2nd ed. 1938). Denver, Colo.

FEDER, NORMAN
1962 Plains Indian Metalworking, with emphasis on hair plates. American Indian Tradition, v. 8, no. 2, pp. 55–76. (Note: had important influence on Navajo silver)
1962 Plains Indian Metalworking, Part II. American Indian Tradition, v. 8, no. 3, pp. 93–108.

FELLIN, OCTAVIA
1959 Ambrose Roanhorse, Peshlakai Natani: Navajo silversmith. Indian Life, Gallup Inter-Tribal Indian Ceremonial Assoc. (Aug.)

FIRESTONE, MELVIN and RODRIGUEZ, ANTONIO
1970 Notes on the derivation of the *naja.* Plateau, v. 42, no. 4, Spring 1970, pp. 139–145.

HEGEMANN, ELIZABETH COMPTON
1962 Navajo Silver (Part I and II). Masterkey, v. 36, no. 2, pp. 45–49; v. 36, no. 3, pp. 102–113.

HILL, GERTRUDE F.
1938 Use of Turquoise among the Navajo. The Kiva, v. 4, no. 3.

HUNT, W. BEN
1952 Indian Silversmithing. Milwaukee: Bruce Publ. Co.

MATTHEWS, WASHINGTON
1968 Navajo Weavers and Navajo Silversmiths. Reprinted from 3rd Ann. Report, B.A.E.. 1881–82, and 2nd Ann. Report, B.A.E., 1880–81. Filter Press, Palmer Lake, Colo. 37 pp. illus.

MERA, HARRY P.
1959 Indian Silverwork of the Southwest, Illustrated. Vol. I. Globe, Ariz.: Dale Stuart King.

MORRISSEY, FRANK R.
1968 Turquoise Deposits of Nevada. Nevada Bureau of Mines Report 17.

NEUMANN, DAVID L.
1971 Navajo Silversmithing, a collection of six articles written 1932–1954. Santa Fe, El Palacio, vol. 77, no. 2, April 1971.

POTTER, CAROLE A.
1964 The Dean Kirk Ketoh Collection. Plateau, v. 36, no. 4, pp. 115–119.

TANNER, CLARA LEE
1954 Navajo Silver Craft. Arizona Highways, v. 30, no. 8, August, pp. 16–33.
1960 Contemporary Southwest Indian Silver. Kiva, v. 25, no. 3, pp. 1–22.
1968 Southwest Indian Craft Arts. Tucson: Univ. of Ariz. Press.

VAN VALKENBURGH, RICHARD
1941 John Lorenzo Hubbell (his role in introducing the Navajos to silverwork). *In* Dine Bekeyah, Window Rock, Ariz.: U.S.D.I., Navajo Service.

WOODWARD, ARTHUR
1944 Romance of Navajo Silver. Arizona Highways, vol. 20, no. 3 (March).
1953 Navajo Silver comes of age. Los Angeles County Museum Quarterly, vol. 10, no. 1, Spring 1953, p. 9–14.

INDEX

About the Author

ARTHUR WOODWARD is a noted historian and archaeologist whose interest in the American Indian began as a youth in his native Iowa and Southern California. During the 1920s he was on the staff of the Heye Foundation's Museum of the American Indian in New York City, and following this, spent twenty-five years as the curator of history and anthropology at the Los Angeles County Museum. He has been a member of numerous archaeological expeditions ranging from Arizona to Alaska, and during World War II accompanied Rear Admiral Richard E. Byrd on a special presidential mission to the South Sea Islands. In the 1960s he gave seminars in historical archaeology at the University of Arizona in Tucson and Texas Christian University, Fort Worth. He now makes his home in Patagonia, Arizona.

NAVAJO SILVER: *A Brief History of Navajo Silversmithing,* originally published in 1938, has become a true classic in its field. It was the first book to present a comprehensive view of the four major influences on Navajo silver design, showing how the early Navajo silversmiths adapted art forms of European settlers and Indians in the eastern United States as well as those of the Spanish and Mexican colonists in the Southwest. This newly designed edition faithfully preserves the original text.